CHARLES BUR

RAILWAY SIGNALMAN OF CROMFORD

INTRODUCTION

Charles Burling, a career railwayman, was born at Lode near Cambridge on 3rd March 1881. The family later settled at nearby Stow cum Quy, but at some time prior to the turn of the century Charles moved to the Barnsley area and in the 1901 census was one of two boarders living with 71 year old widow Mary Osborne at 53 Hough Lane, Wombwell. A few months prior to this – on 5th June 1900 – he had joined the Midland Railway as a porter at Elsecar & Hoyland station, so perhaps he had moved to the area primarily to secure employment. However, as we shall see, he spent much of his career as a signalman, retiring in September 1947, a few weeks before the railways were nationalised.

After covering a variety of jobs, Charles was transferred to Cromford Sidings signal box in Derbyshire just before his 30th birthday in February 1911 and lived in the village for the remainder of his life, although from 1923 to 1938 he worked as a Relief Signalman in the area, and finished his railway career as a signalman at Matlock Bath.

This publication is primarily based on two notebooks compiled by Charles, which have been handed down to his grandsons Roger and John Howe via Frank Burling, Charles' son and their uncle, who lived in Cromford for all but the first three years of his life and died in May 1998 at the age of 90. I am indebted to Roger and John for the loan of the notebooks – and to my wife Angela for initially transcribing the information. Others who have helped are mentioned opposite.

As a coincidence, Frank Burling was my godfather and I can vaguely remember Charles. It is a matter of regret that I was unaware of Charles' railway connections until contacted by Roger about the notebooks after Frank's death. If I had been aware of this, no doubt Frank would have been able to provide me with more concise answers to some of the questions that have arisen from perusing the information in the notebooks.

The two notebooks do not run consecutively, nor do they cover the whole of Charles' adult life – but it is not difficult to determine the salient features of his railway career. Fortunately, both summarise what he did in earlier years. The first book was started in 1912, soon after he came to Cromford, and runs until the end of 1917. It records events in some detail, including both the local and national scene generally. Consequently not all of this concerned railways.

The second notebook was started in 1925 and runs until the end of his railway career in 1947. This notebook, however, is much less detailed. In fact, it almost entirely covers his railway career. It repeats details of his early railway career but, fortunately, also includes his movements between the end of the first book in 1917 and the start of the later one in 1925.

The publication has been produced as a chronology, split into three parts. The first deals with Charles' railway career, while the second one covers the local railway scene between 1912 and 1917, much of which was during wartime. The third part gives details of some general circulars and notices relating to Midland Railway operations and the National Union of Railwaymen, of which Charles was an active member. Inevitably, there is a little overlapping in certain instances.

Some of the information contained in the notebooks led to further research using local newspapers and other sources. Additional commentary is made in certain instances using square brackets, though cases where more detail was found are included as appendices. On the other hand, there are entries where the exact circumstances are unclear. Such entries have been included in this publication as they could well provide readers with information for their own researches.

Glynn Waite – June 2007.
113 Green Oak Road, Totley, Sheffield, S17 4FS.
Tel: 0114-2364728 – Email: Glynn.Waite@btinternet.com

1. Charles' Railway Career

Note that during the period from 1912 to 1917 the details are more comprehensive than at any other period due to the records Charles kept during that time.

05.06.1900 Joined the Midland Railway as a porter at Elsecar & Hoyland.

[Note that his grade was shown as 'porter' in both notebooks rather than 'station porter' as in the entries below. It is possible that he was taken on in a probationary role and covered both passenger and goods duties initially.]

18.03.1901 Removed to Wombwell as station porter.

29.03.1901 Took charge at Wombwell. Received an advance in wages.

[One of the features of railway employment until fairly recent times was that a person rarely took over a new position without first having a period of training]

Left: Elsecar & Hoyland station looking towards Barnsley c.1910. The station was a late addition to the Midland Railway's system, having opened on 1st July 1897 less than three years before Charles started his railway career.

Right: Wombwell station, which also opened on 1st July 1897, looking towards Sheffield, probably around 1905 – the poster on the waiting room wall on the Down platform is advertising the steamer services from Heysham Harbour (opened 1904) to the Isle of Man and Northern Ireland. Note the Booking Office at the top of the slope to the Down platform in the centre right, and the signalbox on the Up platform, which was not a common practice. No doubt Charles' interest in signalling began here due to the proximity of the structure and what would have been an everyday association with the signalmen.

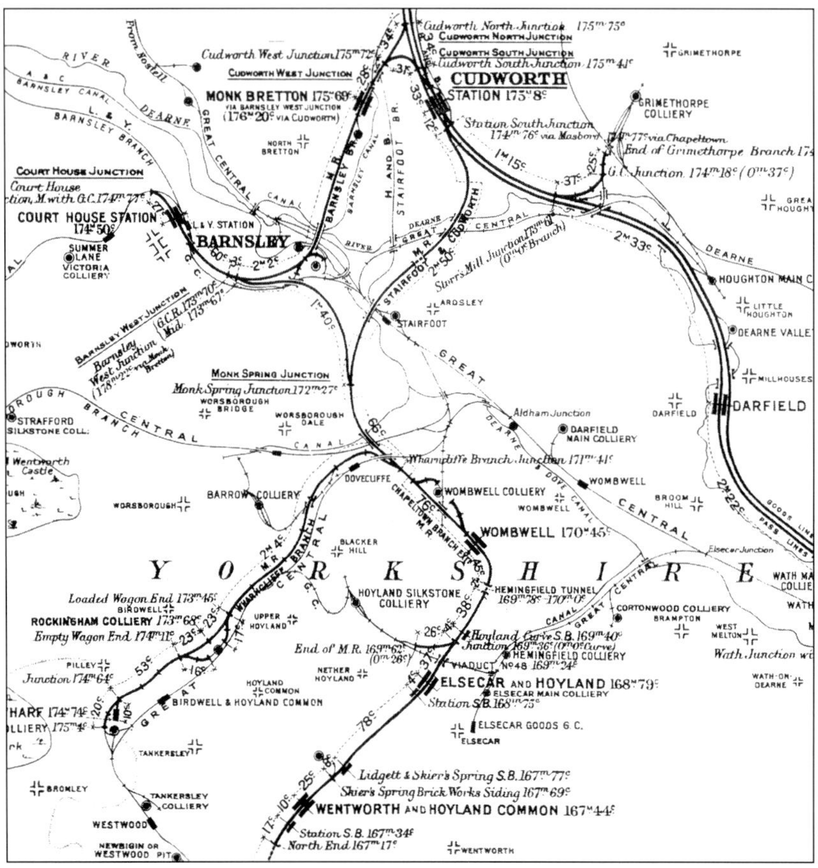

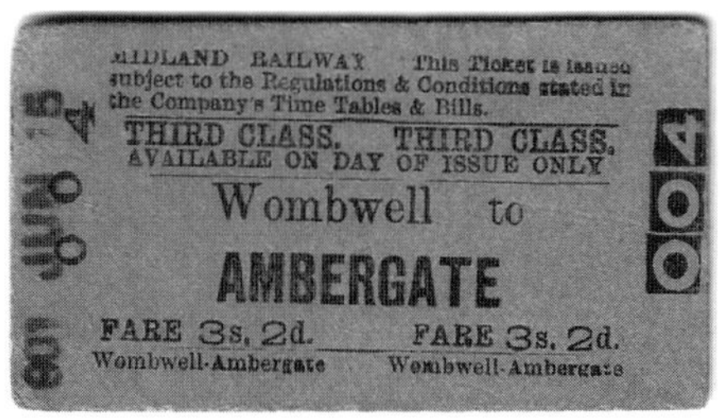

Above: A 3rd Class single from Wombwell to Ambergate issued on 15th June 1901 soon after Charles became a porter at the station. He may well have issued it himself! As a co-incidence, Charles' railway career would take him to Ambergate just over 4 years later. This was obviously not a common journey, as it would appear to be only the fifth ticket issued since the station opened.

Left: An extract from the Midland Railway's distance diagram of the Barnsley area in 1919 showing the position of Elsecar & Hoyland and Wombwell stations. Note the complex of lines and the number of collieries As well as the direct route from Barnsley to Sheffield via these two stations, it was also possible for Barnsley passengers to use the original route, which entailed a change of trains at Cudworth.

SHEFFIELD, CHAPELTOWN, and BARNSLEY.

		WEEKDAYS.															SUNDAYS.		
						Will run from July 20th to September 7th. Sats. only.		Saturdays only.						Wednesdays and Thursdays excepted.	Weds. & Thurs. only.	Saturdays only.			
London (St. Pancras) (For Chapeltown Line.)	dep	11 55	.....	....	5 15	.....	.....	9 0	9 30	12 15	2 10	3 0	4 0	5 45	.....	.....	.....	.....	4 0
Leicester	,,	2A23	..	..	7 20		9 25	10 30	11 35	1 42	3 35	4 35	6 13	7 30	..	..	..	..	5 20
Nottingham	,,	12 0	.....	.....	7 35		9 42	11 29	11 40	2 51	4 37	5 37	6 12	8 22	.....	....	6 25	.....	6 35
Birmingham	,,	11 25	4A15	..	6 5		8 55	..	11 30	2 15	2 55	4B25	5 45	7 15	7 15	..	4 15	..	4 0
Derby	,,	3A10	5A50	.....	8 0		10 7	11 10	12 42	3 17	4 10	5B35	7 10	8 17	8 35	9 20	7 10	.....	6 50
Chesterfield	,,	3A44	7 5	..	8 47		10 52	12 14	1 18	4 3	4 52	6 20	7 52	8 52	9 37	10 30	8 5	..	7 30
		a.m.	a.m	a.m.	a.m.	a.m.	a.m.	p.m.	p.m.	p.m.	p.m.	p.m.	p.m.	p.m.	p.m	p.m.	a.m.	p.m.	p.m.
SHEFFIELD	dep.	**6 50**	**8 10**	..	**9 33**	*10 25*	**11 30**	*1 8*	**1 49**	**4 30**	**6 5**	**6 50**	**8 52**	*10 10*	*11 0*	*11 30*	**9 5**	**2 5**	**8 45**
Attercliffe Road		6 53	8 13	.....	9 36	.....	11 33	*1 11*	1 52	4 33	6 8	.....	8 55	*10 15*	*11 3*	*11 33*	9 8	2 8	8 48
Brightside		6 58	8 18	..	9 41	..	11 38	*1 16*	1 58	4 39	6 14	..	9 0	*10 20*	*11 8*	*11 38*	9 13	2 13	8 53
Ecclesfield		7 6	8 26	.....	9 49	..	11 46	*1 24*	2 6	4 48	6 21	7 1	9 7	*10 28*	*11 16*	*11 46*	9 21	2 21	9 0
Chapeltown		**7 10**	**8 30**	**8 57**	**9 53**	*10 39*	**11 50**	*1 28*	**2 10**	**4 53**	**6 25**	**7 4**	**9 11**	*10 32*	*11 20*	*11 50*	**9 25**	**2 25**	**9 4**
Wentworth and Hoyland Common		7 14	8 34	J	9 57	*10 43*	11 54	*1 32*	2 14	4 57	6 29	7 8	9 15	*10 36*	*11 24*	*11 54*	9 29	2 29	9 8
Elsecar and Hoyland		**7 18**	**8 38**	**9 3**	**10 1**	*10 47*	**11 58**	*1 36*	**2 18**	**5 1**	**6 33**	**7 12**	**9 19**	*10 40*	*11 28*	*11 58*	**9 33**	**2 33**	**9 12**
Wombwell		7 23	8 43	9 8	10 8	.....	12 5	*1 41*	2 2[illegible]	5 6	6 38	7 17	9 24	*10 45*	*11 33*	*12 5*	9 38	2 38	9 17
BARNSLEY	arr.	**7 35**	**8 55**	..	**10 19**	..	**12 13**	*1 53*	**2 33**	**5 20**	**6 48**	**7 20**	**9 34**	*10 57*	*11 45*	*12 15*	**9 50**	**2 50**	**9 26**
Barnsley	dep.	7 40	.....	.....	11C30	.....	12 53	*2 20*	2 55	.....	.....	7 40	9 40	.....	.....	.....	.....	3 0	.....
Cudworth	arr.	7 51	..	9 17	11C40	*10 59*	1 4	*2 31*	3 6	..	..	7 51	..	..	..	..	..	3 10	..
Cudworth	dep.	8 6	.....	9 40	11C47	*11 47*	1 11	*2 38*	3 39	.....	.....	8 3	.....	.....	.....	.....	.....	3 19	.....
Leeds	arr.	9 10	..	10 18	12C20	*12 20*	1 50	*3 10*	4 37	..	..	9 5	10 40	..	..	..	..	4 15	..

		WEEKDAYS.															SUNDAYS.		
		Mondays only, Bank Holidays excepted.	Mondays only, Bank Holidays excepted.							Saturdays only.					Mondays and Saturdays only.				
Leeds	dep	..	*6 15*	..		7 0	8 50	10 25	11 30	..	12 50	4 45	7 6	8 26	..	7 0	2 0	..
Cudworth	arr.	.....	*6 44*	.....		8 0	9 32	10 57	12 22	.....	1 39	5 25	7 56	.....	....	7 58	2 59	.....
Cudworth	dep.	..	*6 46*	..		8 10	9 38	11 8	12 32	..	2 42	5 33	8 5	..	..	8 5	3 15	..
Barnsley	arr.	.....	.....	.....		8 25	9 48	11 18	12 42	.....	2 52	5 43	8 15	9 25	.....	8 15	3 25	.....
		a.m.	a.m.	a.m.		a.m.	a.m.	a.m.	p.m.	p.m.	p.m.	p.m.	p.m.	p.m.	p.m.	a.m.	p.m.	p.m.
BARNSLEY	dep.	*6 27*	..	**7 45**		**8 30**	**10 0**	**11 48**	**1 15**	*2 15*	**3 5**	**5 50**	**8 25**	**9 50**	*11 23*	**10 0**	**4 45**	**9 40**
Wombwell		*6 37*	.....	7 55		8 38	10 8	11 58	1 25	*2 24*	3 13	5 58	8 35	10 0	*11 33*	10 10	4 53	9 50
Elsecar and Hoyland		*6 42*	..	**8 0**		**8 43**	**10 13**	**12 3**	**1 30**	*2 29*	**3 17**	6 2	**8 40**	**10 5**	*11 38*	**10 15**	**4 58**	**9 55**
Wentworth and Hoyland Common		*6 46*	.....	8 4		8 47	10 17	12 7	1 34	*2 34*	3 22	6 6	8 44	10 9	*11 42*	10 19	5 2	9 59
Chapeltown		*6 50*	*7 0*	**8 8**		**8 50**	**10 21**	**12 11**	**1 38**	*2 39*	**3 27**	**6 10**	**8 48**	**10 13**	*11 46*	**10 23**	**5 6**	**10 3**
Ecclesfield		[illegible]	.....	8 12		.....	10 25	12 15	1 42	*2 44*	3 31	**6 14**	8 52	10 17	*11 50*	10 27	5 10	10 7
Brightside		..	..	8 20		..	10 34	12 24	1 51	*2 54*	3 39	6 21	9 0	10 25	*11 59*	10 35	5 17	10 15
Attercliffe Road		.....	.....	8 24		.....	10 40	12 30	1 55	*3 0*	3 45	6 27	9 4	10 29	*12 3*	10 39	5 23	10 19
SHEFFIELD	arr.	..	*7 15*	**8 29**		..	**10 43**	**12 35**	**2 2**	*3 3*	**3 48**	**6 30**	**9 10**	**10 35**	*12 10*	**10 45**	**5 26**	**10 25**
Chesterfield (From Chapeltown Line.)	arr.	.....	7 43	9D23	9 39	.....	11 35	1 19	2 28	3 35	4B18	7 1	10 0	11 40	.....	12 57	6 12	11 42
Derby	,,	..	..	10D0	10 27	..	12 20	1 52	3E 7	4 8	5 55	8 10	..	12 30	..	2 0	9 32	12 20
Birmingham	,,	.....	.....	11D5	11 35	.....	1 24	3 2	4E35	5 20	7 10	11 30	.....	2 7	.....	3 30	11 20	2 7
Nottingham	,,	..	8 29	..	10 23	..	1 7	2 35	3 22	..	5B1	7 46	..	1 37	..	2 52	8 45	1 37
Leicester	,,	.....	9 20	.. ..	11 17	.....	12B17	3 25	3 35	.....	6B2	.....	.....	1 39	.....	2 20	9 0	1 39
London (St. Pancras)	,,	..	11 10	..	12 55	..	2B15	5 0	5 [illegible]0	..	7B35	10 30	..	4 20	..	4 40	11 0	4 20

A—Monday Mornings excepted. **B**—Bank Holidays excepted. **C**—On Mondays Passengers leave Barnsley at 11.5, and reach Cudworth at 11.16 and Leeds at 11.50 a.m. **D**—Mondays only (Bank Holidays excepted). **E**—Until July 15th arrives Derby at 4.0 and Birmingham at 5 20 p.m. **J**—Takes up Passengers for Leeds and North there f.

The passenger timetable for July, August and September 1901, showing the service between Sheffield, Chapeltown and Barnsley. Charles was employed at Wombwell station at this time. Note that the service was relatively sparse when compared with today, which would have given Charles plenty of time to associate with the signalmen.

29.03.1902 Received a further advance in wages after 1 year in charge.

23.10.1902 Removed to Rotherham Westgate as station porter.

29.03.1903 Received a further advance in wages.

[This would indicate that his move to Rotherham was not a promotion, but rather a transfer – probably initiated by the Midland Railway. It was his second annual pay rise since taking charge at Wombwell.]

09.1903 Removed to [Rotherham] Masborough as train recorder.

[This was Charles' first appointment in a signal box. Unfortunately the actual box is not identified. It would have been determined that the workload in the box was sufficiently high for the signalman to require assistance. The most cost effective way of providing such assistance would be to employ a lower graded man to enter details of the bell codes and train movements in the block register and let the signalman concentrate on the non-clerical duties.]

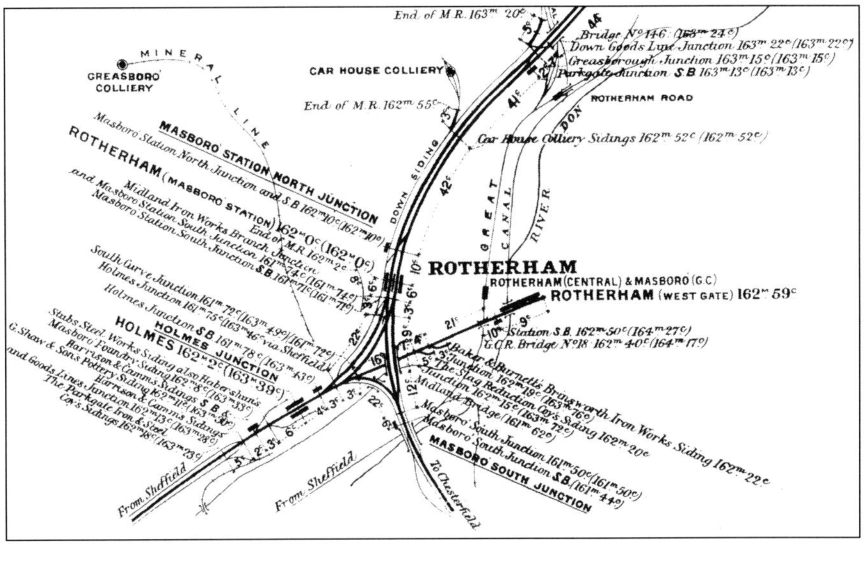

10.1903 Took charge as train recorder.

The signal box in which Charles worked as a train recorder was likely to have been Masborough South Junction. This box, along with Masborough Station South Junction, was replaced by a new structure in the early part of 1903, with the workload possibly increasing. Records show that by 1912 at least the Station South box had an assistant signalman, which would have made the employment of a train recorder less likely in that box. This view of the South Junction box in August 1969, would be little changed from Charles' time in the area.

[M.A. King]

11.04.1904 Removed to Hasland as porter signalman.

[Hasland would appear to have been Charles' base area rather than his actual place of work. The only signal box that bore that name was Hasland Sidings, which was situated on the main line and dealt with locomotives on and off the engine shed. This was too highly graded.

It has not been possible to locate any publication showing the grading of posts at this period in time – but one does exist for 1927, by which time the number of grades had been reduced from 13 to 7 and the post of porter signalman had virtually disappeared[1].

Based on the 1927 listing, perhaps the most likely location was Grassmoor West Junction[2], which bore the prefix Hasland and was in the lowest grade – Class 6. This would have been an ideal 'starting box'. The porter duties could have involved goods work in the adjacent colliery and / or those associated with the colliery workmen's trains[3].]

23.04.1904 Took charge as porter signalman at Hasland. Also received an advance in wages.

02.05.1904 Passed examination at Sheffield.

[The subject was not shown, but in view of his later career, was likely to have been a signalling examination.]

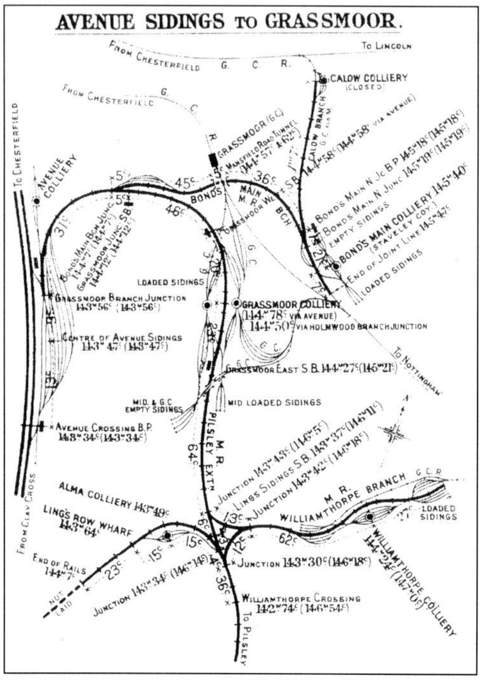

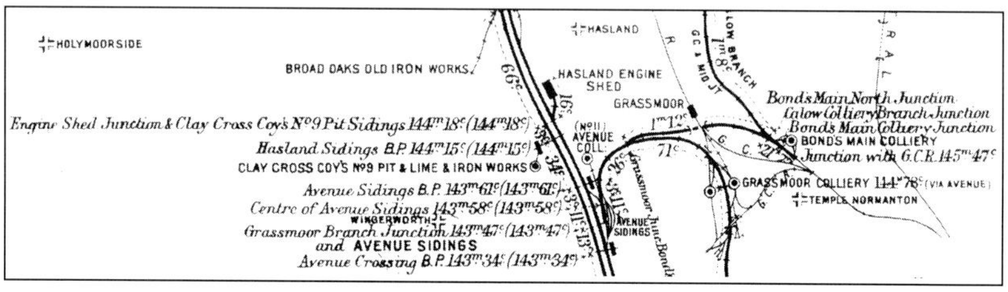

Left: The Avenue Sidings / Grassmoor area in 1909 showing the position of Grassmoor West signal box. The name Hasland does not appear on this diagram, but does appear a couple of times on the one **above**, which also covers the area to the north and east of Avenue Colliery. This shows the position of Hasland Sidings box on the main line and the engine shed on the Up side.

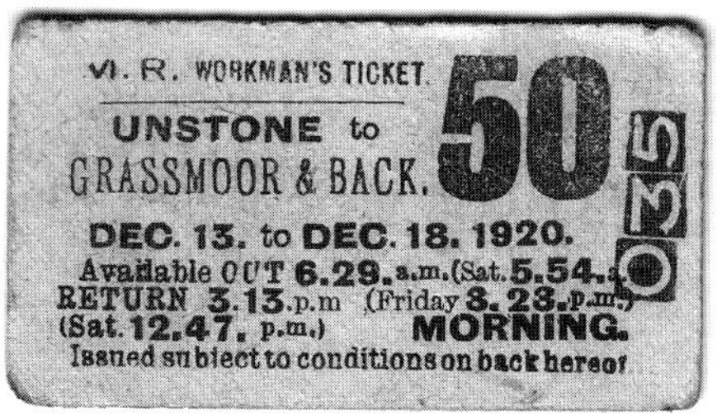

Right: A ticket used by a miner working at Grassmoor Colliery. The trains had to change direction in Avenue Sidings.

1 The agreement that provided for a reduction in the number of grades was signed in March 1920 and applied retrospectively to 1st January. The number of grades were actually reduced to 6 initially, but later increased to 7. See Appendix "D".

2 Closed 3rd September 1934.

3 These operated from c.1874 to 9th November 1927.

26.04.1905 Applied for signalman post at Elsecar [not successful]

[In 1927, this was a Class 5 box and would have been a promotion from his porter signalling duties.]

29.05.1905 Removed to Barrow Hill as signalman.

[Again, the actual signal box was not specified. Based on 1927 gradings, this was likely to have been Summit Sidings[4], which was then a Class 5G (goods only) box. From 1920, signalmen in goods only boxes were paid slightly less than those in the same class who dealt with passenger trains.]

08.06.1905 Passed for box at Barrow Hill and took charge on this date. Also received an advance in wages.

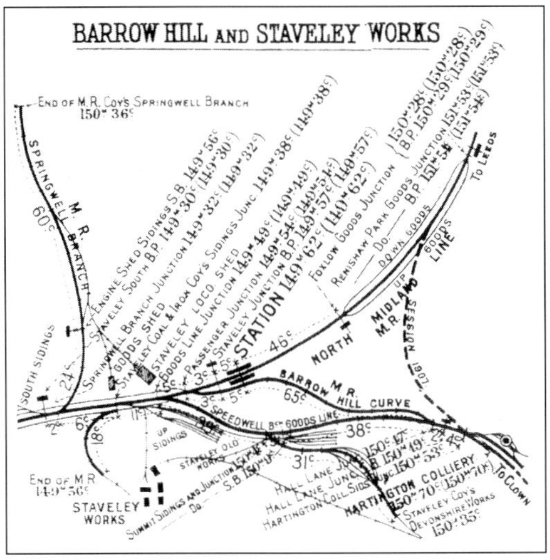

Left: The Barrow Hill area in 1909, with Summit Sidings signal box located in the bottom centre.

Right: Summit Sidings signal box on 25th June 1972, a few months before it closed. It is believed that this is where Charles worked. [M.A. King]

Whit. 1905 Sent to Shipley to assist at Bingley Junction during the Whitsuntide holiday.

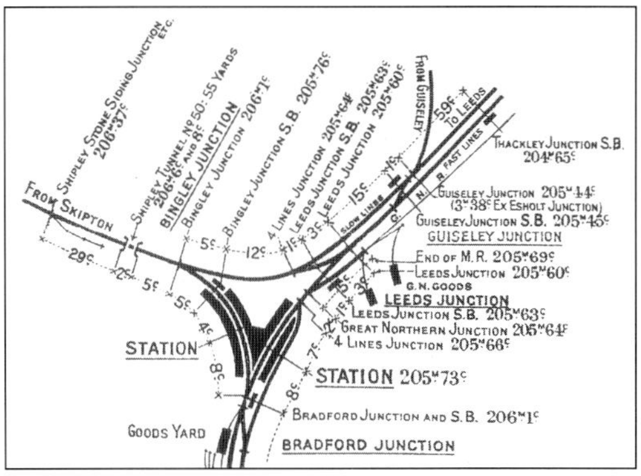

[This box was situated at the west end of the Shipley triangle. This was an interesting arrangement, which indicates that shortages of signalmen at peak times were met by the temporary transfer of men from boxes that were not continuously manned. Summit Sidings was closed between 10.0pm on Saturdays and 6.0am on Mondays, and was unlikely to be manned at Bank Holidays. Men booked off at Bank Holidays at that time were not paid. Charles presumably volunteered to work elsewhere to ensure that he did not lose a day's pay – and also get some Sunday duty. Bingley Junction box does not appear to have been doubled-manned, so Charles would no doubt have required a few hours to 'learn the box' so that he could work it himself]

17.10.1905 Removed to Ambergate as signalman.

[Once again the actual box was not specified. However, in view of a later entry – on 10th November 1906 – that Buckland Hollow[5] box was *'made 10 hours'*, this is probably where he was located. This was a Class 5 box in the 1927 listing and would have resulted in a small increase in his wages. Had he been promoted to the equivalent of a later Class 4 position this would have made his subsequent move to Cromford Sidings a grade to grade transfer – which it certainly wasn't, as he received an advance in wages after taking over. Class 4 boxes at Ambergate were Station Junction, West Junction, Crich Junction (reduced in grade 2nd August 1926), Bull Bridge and Johnson's Sidings. In view of subsequent entries, the reference to *'10 hours'* is believed to relate to the length of the signalmen's turns of duty, and not the box's hours of opening.]

25.10.1905 Passed for box at Ambergate.

[4] This box opened at an unknown date between 1885 and 1888 and closed on 8th April 1973.

[5] The signalbox here replaced an earlier one on 27th April 1902. It closed on 1st September 1963.

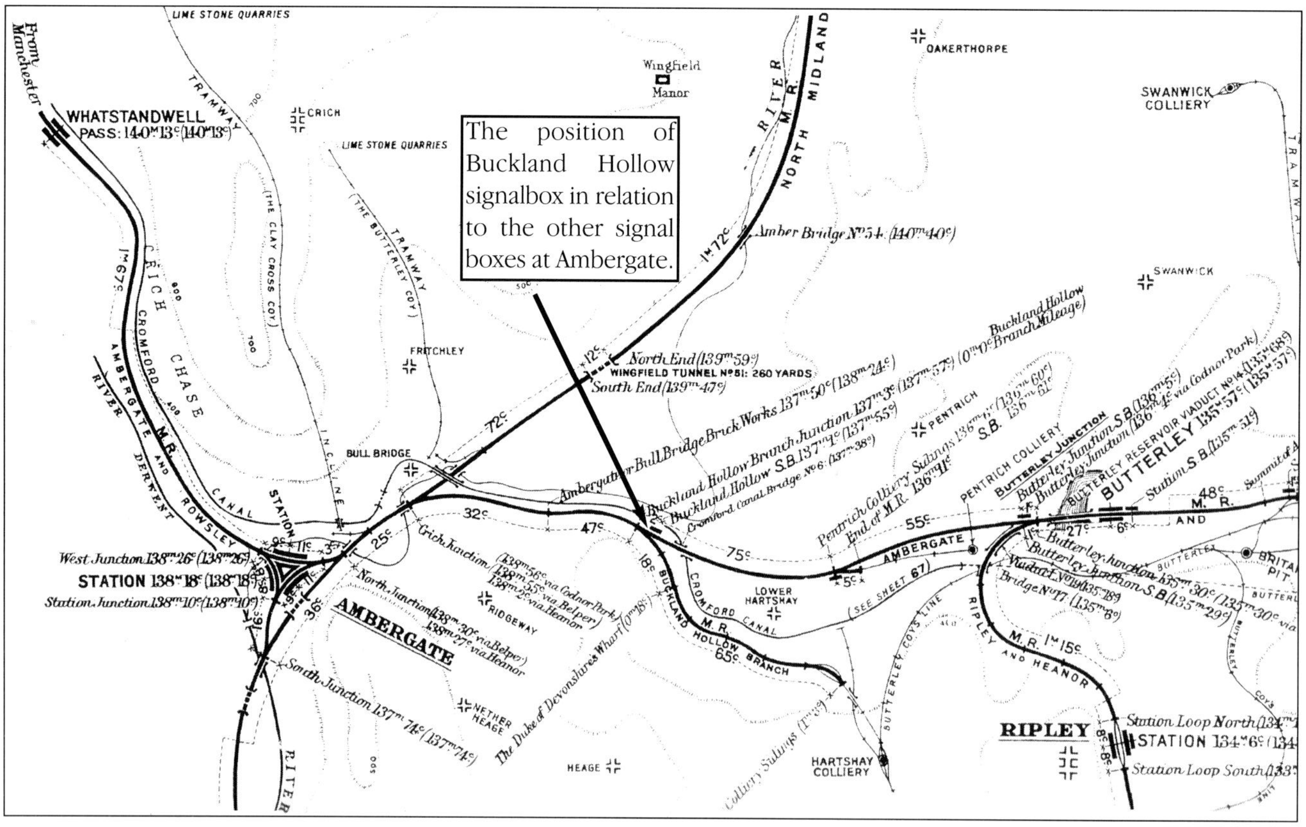

The position of Buckland Hollow signalbox in relation to the other signal boxes at Ambergate.

03.11.1905 Took charge of box at Ambergate. Also received an advance in wages.

06.1909 Asked to accept transfer to signalmen's posts at Cromford Sidings, Rowsley Station and Bakewell.

[Presumably declined a transfer – note that had he transferred to Rowsley Station box he would not have been there for long, as it was closed on 17th April 1910]

22.11.1910 Asked to accept transfer to Cromford Sidings signalbox again.

26.11.1910 Accepted job as signalman Cromford Sidings.

10.02.1911 Removed to Cromford Sidings.

[The signal box, which opened on 1st September 1890, was situated 142 miles 47 chains from St. Pancras, and 43 chains south of Cromford station, at a point where the River Derwent, the railway, and the Cromford Canal are very close together. As well as the signalbox (which was on the Up side of the line), three dead-end recess sidings were also laid on the Down side. Their main use was in regulating freight trains bound for Rowsley and beyond, though there were occasions when empty coaching stock was stabled in the sidings.

An entry in one of Charles' notebooks states *'River bed removed 1884'*. This was connected with a slewing of the lines, which made it possible to lay the three recess sidings and for a signal box to be erected at that point.

Appendix "A" explains some of the early developments relating to Cromford Sidings signal box and signalling arrangements in the area in general.]

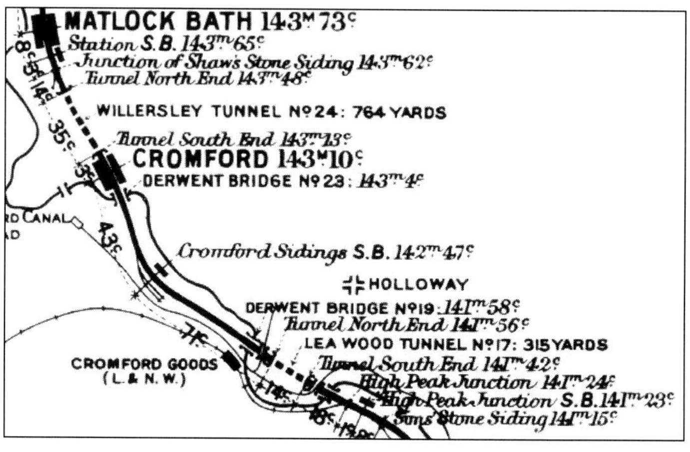

A general view of the Chapel Hill area. Charles and his wife Emma lived in Chapel Hill when they came to Cromford in 1911 and remained there until 1922 when they moved to 6 The Hill.

20.02.1911 Took charge of box at Cromford Sidings. Also received an advance in wages.

27.03.1911 Day's leave for removing from Ambergate. [Charles initially moved to a house in Chapel Hill at Cromford.]

21.06.1911 Asked to accept signalman's post at Millers Dale Lime Co's Sidings. Refused.

08.1911 Advance of 1s.0d per week in wages.

[In 1911 there were a number of meetings of the Midland Railway Conciliation Boards to discuss the grievances of the staff. Most grades were given 1s.0d a week pay rise as an interim measure.]

19.12.1911 Signalmen at Cromford Sidings applied for box to be made 8 hours.

[It will be noted from Appendix "B" that turns of duty could be 8, 9 or 10 hours – also that any man employed for less than a full turn would be paid a full day's wage. The working week actually consisted of 60 hours, which equated to 6 turns of 10 hours. However, there are only 24 hours in a day, so if 10 hour working was in operation, there would be 4 hours to cover. While Charles does not say how this was achieved – he would not mention what were then common practices – it is believed that one of the men at Cromford was a reliefman who covered 4 hours at that box and a similar period at an adjacent box. Other entries indicate that there were three men located at Cromford – hence the application for the box to be made 8 hours. Sunday duty was treated separately and at enhanced rates, while there were further enhancements for working night duty.

The request does not appear to have been conceded – see 13.06.1913]

18.03.1912 Cromford Sidings signal box closed 9.30pm to 7.30am from 18th March to 11th April 1912.

[18th March was a Monday; 11th April was the Thursday after Easter. Cromford Sidings signal box had always been open continuously during the week, but closed on '*Sunday and Sunday night*', prior to this time (the 1913 appendix was more specific, quoting the opening hours as '*6am Monday to 4.20am Sunday*') No reason is given for this change. Perhaps there was a staff shortage – either at Cromford or in the area generally – as the arrangement does not appear to have been repeated.]

01.07.1912 Received an advance of 2s.6d per week under new classification.

02.07.1912 Cromford Sidings in Class 4 under new classifications – 27s.6d per week

[A completely new range of signal box grades was introduced on 1st July 1912. There were still 11 grades, as hitherto, but old grades were combined and new ones introduced. The new grades started at 1 and increased to 11, so Cromford Sidings was at the lower end of the scale. There was no corresponding grade to the new Class 4. However, the fact that Charles received a 2s.6d increase in his wages indicates that his former grade was probably that referred to as '*Second*'. See Appendix "B"]

An idyllic view of Cromford station from a postcard, sent to an address in Mansfield in August 1907. Eleven passengers and either the Station Master or a porter pose on the Up (Derby direction) platform prior to the arrival of a train. It is possibly a Sunday as Willersley Tunnel is unusually clear of smoke. Note the Station Master's house of 1855 and the unique Up side waiting room, which was built 5 years later. The buildings on the Down platform date from 1874. Two turnover levers for the station's signals can be seen near to the overbridge on the Down platform. The post which carried Matlock Bath's inner distant signal can just be seen at the entrance to Willersley Tunnel.

04.1913 Applied for signalman's post at Matlock Bath [not successful]

13.06.1913 Signalmen at Cromford Sidings again applied for box to be made 8 hours [see 29.12.1911]

08.12.1913 Applied for removal to London or Sheffield Districts.

[It would appear that Charles and his family had not yet properly settled in the area and that perhaps a better wage to help raise two children was more important at that time. Frank was born at Ambergate in 1907 and Winnie at Cromford soon after the family moved home.]

11.12.1913 Received acknowledgement of transfer application from General Superintendent – put on list.

13.02.1914 [Received a 1s.0d per week increase in wages under new signalmen's agreement. This was not included in Charles' notebook, although meetings relating to the settlement were. See Section 2 and Appendix "C".]

05.03.1914 Returned one card and ten pence to E. Lake Railway Servants PT Movement per R. Smith [signalman] High Peak Junction.

[see comment under undated entry at start of 1915.]

22.07.1914 Sent letter to Mr J. Taylor. Received reply 25th July 1914 re Mr W. Broakes, c/o Station Master Harringay Park about exchanging boxes. Could not exchange owing to Cromford being 10 hours. Harringay Park 27s.6d plus 3s.0d London rate.

[The circumstances of this application can only be assumed. Perhaps Charles had become aware that a signalman from Harringay Park, in North London, was seeking a mutual exchange of positions and had written about this. It is not known who Mr J. Taylor was – possibly the local signalling supervisor.]

16.08.1914 Cromford Sidings and Matlock signal boxes kept open for protection of tunnels owing to outbreak of war until 26th November 1914.

A subsequent entry stated *'Cromford Sidings box always open from 16th August to 26th November 1914, then closed as usual from 26th November to 27th December 1914*[6]*; always open from 27th December 1914 to October 1916*[7]*'*.

[Details of trains scheduled to be dealt with by the signalmen at Cromford Sidings when the box was first open on Sundays can be found in Appendix "F".]

27.08.1914 Received permit No D 1461.

[This was provided by the Midland Railway and was presumably related to working in a vital industry and not being called up for the war effort. See 13.07.1916 when the permit was returned to the Company.]

6 *'As usual'* meant closed from 4.20am Sunday to 6.0am Monday.

7 A subsequent entry shows the actual date as 8th October.

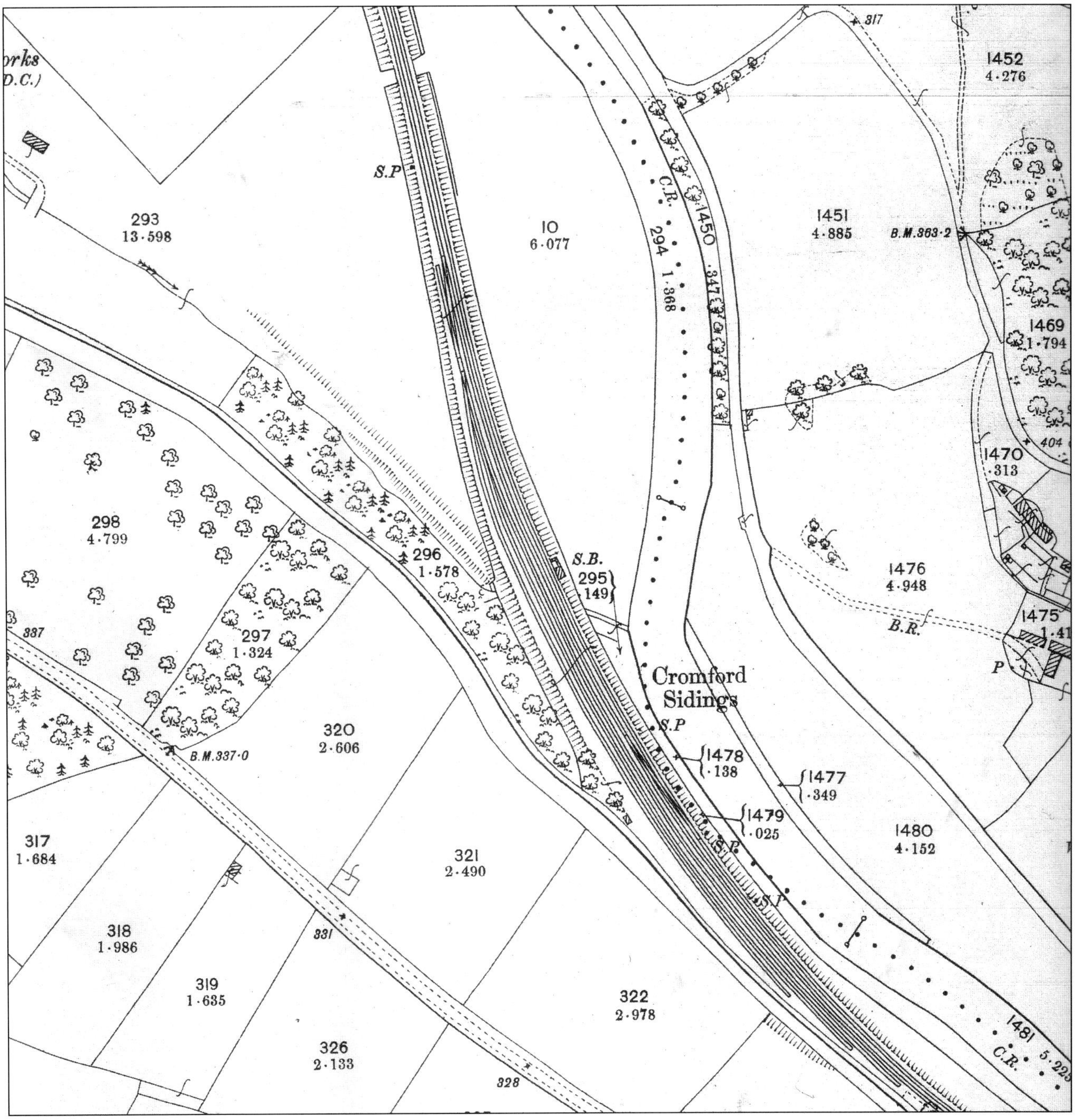

Top: The 25" to a mile OS map for the Cromford Sidings area in 1899, showing the position of the signal box (S.B.) and signal posts (S.P.). Additional comment is made about this map in Appendix "A".

Above left: The route through the Meadows that the signalmen would have taken when walking to and from the box. The Old Baileans rugby headquarters is behind the trees on the right.

Above right: The previous photo was taken from the gate behind the tree in the centre. From here steps can be seen leading up the railway embankment. The signal box was on the opposite side of the line. [Yvonne Daykin]

A photograph of one of Cromford's football teams taken around the time that Charles came to the village, with the top of the signalbox in the background. The path to the box and the steps up the embankment are in the top right. Nowadays, the Old Baileans play rugby in this part of the Meadows.
[Alan Swift collection]

27.12.1914 Cromford Sidings box always open from 27th December 1914 to …….., for removal of troop train.

[As mentioned previously (16.08.1914) a subsequent entry shows the end date as 8th October 1916. The troop train stabled in the sidings would have been empty stock – and, presumably, not the one mentioned on 29.08.1914 (see Section 2). Initially, the box would have had to be manned continuously as the stock could have been called for at any time.]

– Railway Servants Universal Privilege Ticket card for 1915. No. 91782

[This was an arrangement whereby employees of one company – in this case the Midland Railway – were allowed to purchase reduced rate tickets for journeys over participating companies' lines. The employees paid half the ordinary 3rd class single fare, subject to a minimum fare of 3d – although return fares at double the single fare could also be issued. The facilities also extended to wives and children. A privilege ticket order form, which specified the journey to be made, had to be applied for in advance, and was handed to the Booking clerk / porter along with the appropriate fare when the journey was to be made. This type of arrangement continued until the early 1960s.]

06.01.1915 4s 9d short in wages 6th January. Applied for it same day. It is for Sunday 27th December 1914. Received reply from General Superintendent 13th January 1915 – having attention. Received money on 3rd February in pay for week ending 28th January.

11.01.1915 November 1914 issue of clothing arrived today.

13.01.1915 Returned trousers to Derby. Too small round waist.

[Ill fitting clothing was a feature of railway employment – even though the employees submitted measurements on each occasion.]

Paid one shilling to Mr Brown for Casualty Fund. Sheet No C.874.

[Mr Brown was the Station Master at Cromford – see Section 2. The Casualty Fund would no doubt have been connected with the war.]

20.01 1915 Received tie from Midland Railway Co. First one.

[While the Midland Railway provided various pieces of uniform, this did not initially include ties. It is recorded that in late 1911 / early 1912 platform porters at larger stations were requested to wear black ties, which they had to provide at their own expense. The men at Sheffield station objected to this and initially came to work in rainbow coloured ties! By 1913, ties for station staff were being provided by the Company. This entry indicates that the arrangement was later extended to signalmen.]

15.02.1915 Received war bonus of 3s.0d per week (payment from 15th to 20th February received on latter date).

[One of the consequences of the war was that costs began to rise and inflation – a word that few people would have been aware of prior to that time – began to take a hold. Employees in all industries started to receive war bonuses to offset the increased cost of living. These were granted at quite frequent intervals. This was the first occasion that a war bonus was paid to Charles. Other awards are included in the text to the end of 1917.]

20.02.1915 Received November 1914 issue of trousers after being sent to Derby as misfit.

02.06.1915 Paid sixpence to Mr Brown [Station Master] Cromford for Railway Corps in France to get capes etc. for men.

23.06.1915 Received May issue uniform – overcoat No.2582B, serge jacket No.4528, serge vest No.4528, serge trousers, cap and tie.

05.07.1915 Received £1.10s.4d from Midland Railway (from 9th February).

[Presumably back pay, but reason not explained]

15.07.1915 Received war badge No.5605. [This was accompanied by a letter, which had to be signed and read as follows:]

Midland Railway War Badge

Badge No 5605 is issued to C. Burling who is employed as a Signalman in the Coaching Department at Cromford Station.

It is issued on the understanding that the Company is unable to spare him from Railway employment at the present time that he will not transfer it to any other person and that he will surrender it to the Railway if and when called upon to do so on the conditions set out above.

Signed C. Burling

Date July 15th 1915

06.09.1915 [Charles recorded details of how he spent his annual leave starting on this date – as he did on another occasion. Most of the information below is not directly associated with his career, other than the fact that as a railwayman it enabled him to make use of his free passes and reduced fare concessions to visit friends and relations – a practice that could not be enjoyed by workers in other industries. Annual and special leave records maintained elsewhere in his notebook tell us that he only took 5 days leave – from 7th to 11th September. The 6th was a Monday and would have been a working day. It would appear that he went to Sutton after finishing a morning shift on that day. The 13th was the following Monday. His notes tell us that he went to Hoyland during that day, and then started a 12 hour night shift.

All of the Cromford signalmen took their annual leave consecutively during 1915 – R. Willan (see Section 2) from 14th to 18th September – hence the need for Charles to work 12 hour shifts during that week – and G. Weaving from 20th to 24th September. 12 hour working does not appear to have been necessary during that week as a note states *'Reliefman Hart vice Weaving'*.]

6th – Went to Sutton [Surrey] via St Pancras on 2.24pm train from Cromford.
7th – Epsom Downs and back to Sutton.
8th – Sutton to London. Seen results of air raid at Bermondsey and went to Tower and St Paul's. Then from St Pancras to Quy [via Kettering and Midland Railway line to Cambridge].
11th – Quy to Cromford.
13th – Cromford to Hoyland and back.

Started work 13th September on nights – 12 hours working.

11.10.1915 Received 2s.0d per week war bonus from this date, making 5s.0d per week.

06.11.1915 Received card to join Army Reserve.

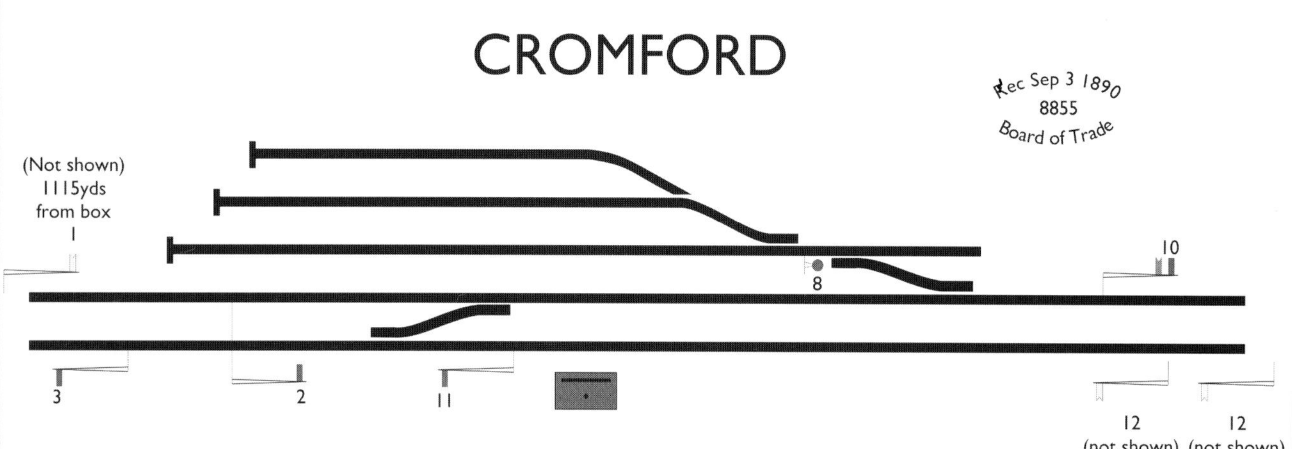

A diagram of the signalling layout at Cromford Sidings when first opened in September 1890.
[drawn by Dave Harris from the original plan – MT6/524/5.]

12.11.1915 Went to Derby to pass Doctor for Army Reserve. Passed for active service at home and abroad and placed in Group M.17. Card No.10.

03.12.1915 Received trousers and tie – November issue.

05.01.1916 Paid one shilling to Mr Brown [Station Master] for casualty fund.

10.05.1916 Letter received from General Superintendent's Office, Midland Railway, Derby, as follows:.

Calling up of Army Reserve Group 33 to 41.

Please inform Signalman C. Burling that we cannot at present release him from his railway duties and that it will not be necessary for him to report himself at the Recruiting Office on May 29th the date on which Groups 33 to 41 are called up. You will be advised if and when he can be liberated. If he should receive a notice paper from the Military authorities this must be forwarded to me, and he must continue at his railway duties.

For General Superintendent. Mr Brown.

13.05.1916 Received May issue of clothing. Serge jacket Class No.3671/3928, Serge waistcoat, serge trousers, cap and black tie.

13.06.1916 Paid 1s.0d to Guard W. Hinton, Derby for Railway Employees Self Help Society to Convalescent Homes; ticket No. 17 dated March 1916.

[Guard Hinton is believed to have been based at Derby]

A Rowsley bound goods train proceeds along Cromford Meadows at an unknown date, but probably in the late 1950s. The signal box is hidden behind the trees on the right, but the end of the sidings can be seen near the train's brakevan. Cromford Sidings' Down starting signal can just be made out a little to the left of the brakevan, while Cromford station is obscured by the trees on the far left.

20.06.1916 Military papers received [calling Charles] to report at Bakewell on 5th July under the Military Service Act 1916. Military Regiment No 6. Placed in Class 40.

Papers sent to General Superintendent's Office, Derby same day.

Reply received on 22nd June, which read as follows:

Calling up of Groups 33 to 41 : Signalman C. Burling.

Burling cannot at present be released to join the Forces and must therefore continue at his Railway duties pending the receipt of further instructions from this office. We have retained the notice paper.

for General Superintendent.

20.06.1916 Received card from Midland Railway Company. Copy below:

Midland Railway Co. 17th June 1916.

To C. Burling, Coaching Dept, Cromford Station.

You are hereby informed that your services are required in connection with the working of the Railway, you will not therefore, at present be required to join the army but should you receive a notice calling you up, you should report to the Recruiting Officer who has sent you the notice, and show him this card, give him any particulars he may require, and ask him to communicate with the Railway Company if he has any doubts. This card has been issued with the approval of the War Office.

Signature of authorised Officer, J.H. Follows, Derby.

13.07.1916 Permit No D1461 handed back to Midland Railway Co.

[This permit was given to Charles on 27th August 1914 (see entry for that date). It was probably returned as he had received a war badge from the company on 15th July 1915 and 'armlet No.F44759 from Matlock' on 7th January 1916. While this may not have been railway related, it was presumably a further way of identifying that he was covering a job that was essential to the war effort.]

13.09.1916 (and on 14th, 19th and 20th September) General Managers of the Railways met the National Union of Railwaymen officials concerning advance of wages. 5s.0d war bonus granted making 10s.0d – war bonus to be paid from 11th September 1916.

08.10.1916 Finished Sunday work.

[This ties in with the entry for 16.08.1914, which states that the signalbox was '*always open from 27th December 1914 to October 1916*']

13.12.1916 Applied for the vacancy of Reliefman. Acknowledged 15th December – having attention.

For eight days from 23rd April 1968 tests were carried out on the line to assess the braking capabilities of Continental ferry wagons fitted with the P4 Westinghouse air brake, with some trains conveying as many as 100 vehicles. These two photos show one of the trains passing the site of the by now closed Cromford Sidings. The engine in the photo on the left has just passed the site of the signal box, while the end of the train cannot be seen and may still be in Willersley Tunnel! Note the curvature of the track and the telegraph poles on the right of the train, which were a common feature of railways at that time.

08.03.1917 Paid one shilling to Guard Hinton for Railway employees Self Help Society to Convalescent Homes.

17.03.1917 Received 'train divided' signal from Matlock Bath for 2.45am Rowsley to Derby. Engine 3269. Guard Partridge of Rowsley.

[The 2.45am from Rowsley was a 'Through Freight' to St. Marys, which was scheduled to run non-stop, so a coupling presumably broke en route. Charles does not comment on the delay incurred. No report of this incident has been found in the local newspapers, presumably because it occurred during the night time and did not affect the running of passenger services.

Engine 3269 entered service as No.1942 in 1891. It was renumbered 3269 in 1907. It should have become 43269 at Nationalisation, but only lasted a few months into the BR era, being withdrawn in May 1948. The engine was allocated to Buxton at this time, and presumably outbased at Rowsley.]

09.04.1917 5s.0d war bonus per week granted to wages staff and one sixth for Sunday duty.

17.05.1917 Asked for reply to application for Reliefman [see 13.12 1916]. Received reply 23rd May 1917:

Please inform Burling the vacancy at Rowsley is not being filled up at present. When it does his claim for promotion will be considered with others.

22.11.1917 NUR E.C. met Railway Executive for advance of wages. RE offered 5s.0d per week; refused by NUR officials.

30.11.1917 Following further meetings, agreement reached on war bonuses as follows:

Male employees 18 years and up – 6s.0d;
Boys under 18 – 3s.0d;
Female employees 18 years and up – 3s.0d;
Female employees under 18 – 1s.6d.

[This is the last record in Charles' notebooks relating to war bonuses. He was now receiving 21s.0d bonus per week on top of his basic wage of 28s.6d. Further bonuses would be granted in the following years as the level of inflation did not reach its peak until January 1921 – at 169% above the pre-war 'cost of living' – and then only reduced gradually.]

01.1918 Summary of wages received [during Charles' time at Cromford Sidings]:

1st July to 31st December 1911	£34.16s.5d
1st January to 31st December 1912	£72.15s.4d
1st January to 31st December 1913	£72. 0s.0d
1st January to 31st December 1914	£86.15s.8d
1st January to 31st December 1915	£105. 5s.5d
1st January to 31st December 1916	£113. 3s.5d
1st January to 31st December 1917	£121. 7s.4d

Cromford Station and Meadows from the top of Willersley Tunnel c.1935. Unfortunately, the signal box is obscured by a tree, but its approximate position is arrowed. By this time Matlock Bath's Down distant signal and Cromford Sidings' Up distant signal were on one post at the end of the Down platform (see Appendix "A"). The tents on the right are part of a school camp.

[The following features recorded on preceding pages would have had an effect on the wages Charles received during this period:

To August 1911 – paid 24s.0d per week.
From August 1911 – 25s.0d per week.
From 1st July 1912 – 27s.6d per week.
From 13th February 1914 – 28s.6d per week (basic wage)
16th August 1914 to 26th November 1914 – signal box open on Sundays.
27th December 1914 to 8th October 1916 – signal box open on Sundays.
From 15th December 1915 – 3s.0d per week war bonus (cost of living).
From 11th October 1915 – Additional 2s.0d per week war bonus (5s.0d in total).
From 1st September 1916 – Additional 5s.0d per week war bonus (10s.0d in total).
From 9th April 1917 – Additional 5s.0d per week war bonus (15s.0d in total).
From 30th November 1917 – Additional 6s.0d per week war bonus (21s.0d in total).

08.1918 Asked to accept position at Rowsley North Junction – declined.

01.02.1919 [While nothing was recorded in either of Charles' notebooks, it is relevant to note that the 8-hour day / 48 hour working week was conceded on this day. This would have made a significant difference to the working arrangements at Cromford Sidings and other signal boxes in the area.]

13.11.1920 Applied for post of Relief signalman at Derby. Received reply 16th November 1920. [subsequently unsuccessful]

Left: On 27th January 1922, Charles and Emma moved from Chapel Hill to 6 The Hill, Cromford. This was rented from the Willersley Estates for 10s.6d per month – which indicates that the property at Chapel Hill was also rented (a common feature in those days). Shortly afterwards houses and land owned by the Willersley Estates were sold, some by auction and some to sitting tenants. Charles was therefore able to purchase his home – a price of £85 being agreed in June 1924. This photo shows Emma and a young John Swift – a member of a family long associated with Cromford, who was born in 1931 – in front of their new house.

[Roger Howe collection]

Above: Charles and Emma in their garden at 6 The Hill, probably taken in the mid-1930s.

[John Howe collection]

10.05.1922 Asked to accept position at Rowsley South Junction – declined.

11.05.1922 Asked to accept position at Buxton Station signalbox – declined.

29.06.1922 Asked to accept position of Relief signalman. [Reaction not recorded, but see entries for 1923].

08.01.1923 Examination at Derby for Relief signalman post – passed.

10.01.1923 Advised of appointment to post of Relief signalman.

16.04.1923 Finished as Signalman Cromford Sidings.

17.04.1923 Started as District Relief signalman, home station Cromford.

11.03.1926 Finished as District Relief signalman, Cromford.

12.03.1926 Started as District Relief signalman, home station Buxton.

[We can only speculate about this move. The 1927 NUR listing – which was compiled when Charles was at Rowsley (see below) shows that he was then a Class 2 relief Signalman and that he had been in that grade since 17th April 1923, when he was appointed a reliefman at Cromford Sidings. It is possible then that this was a temporary transfer to alleviate staff shortages in the Buxton area during a period of depression when few new recruits were being taken on. If that was the case, then Charles would not have been required to move his home and the London Midland & Scottish Railway (which had been formed on 1st January 1923) would have allowed him to lodge at Buxton when on duty and return home to his family at weekends and on rest days].

24.07.1927 Finished as District Relief signalman, Buxton.

25.07.1927 Started as District Relief signalman, Rowsley.

[NUR records show that Charles covered the Grade 2 relief post at Rowsley (there was also a Special Class reliefman). One of the features of signalling grades was that a Grade 2 reliefman received the same basic rate as Grade 3 signalman in a regular box. Only speculation, of course, but assuming that Charles' move to Buxton was a temporary promotion to alleviate LM&SR staffing problems, then this move would have been a repositioning in the same grade at a location nearer to his home.]

06.10.1927 Copy of letter of this date below – origin not identified:

It is to be understood that Rowsley is the home station of Burling and that travelling time and expenses will be calculated accordingly, and also it is expected that he will remove to Rowsley

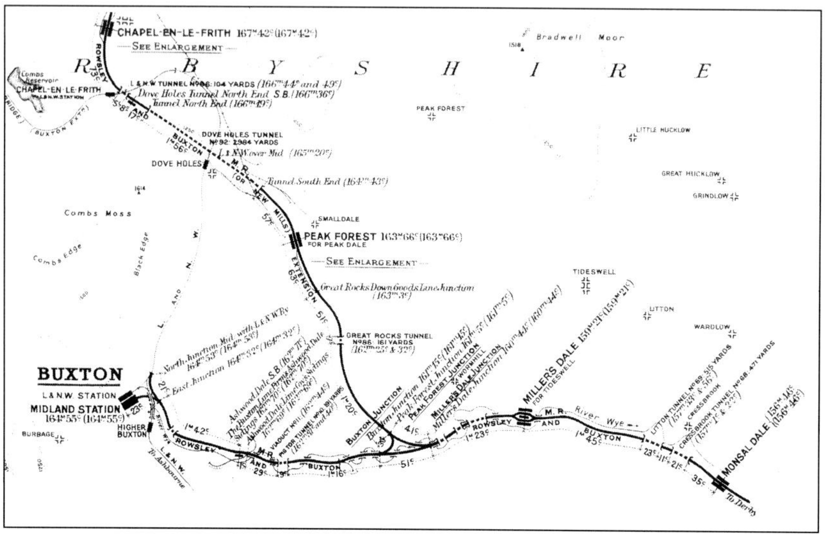

Left: An extract from the Midland Railway's distance diagram of the Buxton area showing some of the signal boxes Charles would have relieved at.

Right: When Charles went to Rowsley in July 1927, he would have relieved at various signal boxes between Hassop and Darley Dale. At that time, there was only one box in Rowsley Down Sidings, but in the same month of his transfer, it was decided to extend the Sidings and add another signal box. He would have witnessed the various works, which were brought into use in September 1928. Rowsley Down Sidings No.2 box is in the centre of this photograph, with the No.1 box on the far right. The coach on the left is on a road leading to a small turntable.

without delay, pending which he must make complete arrangements to fill the requirements of his position.

[It is obvious that while Charles was based at Rowsley, he was not living nearby, and was presumably travelling daily from Cromford. The tone of the letter indicates that he could have been claiming for travelling time and expenses as though based at Cromford. Nothing further is recorded about this matter and it is certain that he did not move his home to Rowsley, so presumably he travelled to most of his relieving locations in his own time – a bicycle being the usual mode of transport for those who had to get to and from work at times when there was no public transport.]

25.10.1933 Finished as District Relief signalman, Rowsley.

26.10.1933 Continued as District Relief signalman.

[Based on the next entry, it is believed that his new home station was Matlock Bath – a far more convenient location to his home.]

10.04.1938 Finished on relief work at Matlock Bath (Sunday).

11.04.1938 Started as signalman Matlock Bath. Seniority date 22nd March 1938.

[Charles is now 57 and had possibly had enough of the travelling and irregular hours associated with relief work and wished to settle down in a job where he knew exactly what he was doing and when.]

20.10.1941 Eyesight test at Derby. [Possibly a late age 60 test]

09.03.1946 65 years of age. Retained over age.
Received pension of 10s.0d per week.

20.09.1947 Finished work [at Matlock Bath] this day.

27.09.1947 Received 7s.0d per week from LMS Club.

02.10.1947 Received full pension of 26s.0d per week.

Traffic Staff—con.

COMPOSITE RATE (Standard Rate plus 28s. war advance).

GRADE.	INDUSTRIAL. s. d.
Signalman, Passenger and Goods—	
Class, Special	114 6
Class 1	108 6
Class 2	103 0
Class 3	97 6
Class 4	93 6
Class 5	89 6
Relief Signalman—	
Class, Special	119 6
Class 1	108 6
Class 2	97 6

London rates 2s. higher, **Rural** rates 1s. lower than above amounts.

Right: The rates of pay for signalmen when Charles retired. Matlock Bath was a Class 4 box.

Matlock Bath station and signalbox c.1890, showing what were originally staggered platforms. The signal box was moved to a position just behind the photographer on 15th March 1891.

Left: A similar view to the photograph at the bottom of page 17, in this case taken c.1910. A number of differences will be noted, as well as the removal of the signal box.

Right: The new 1891 signal box in which Charles worked for the last 9 ½ years of his railway career. [M.A. King]

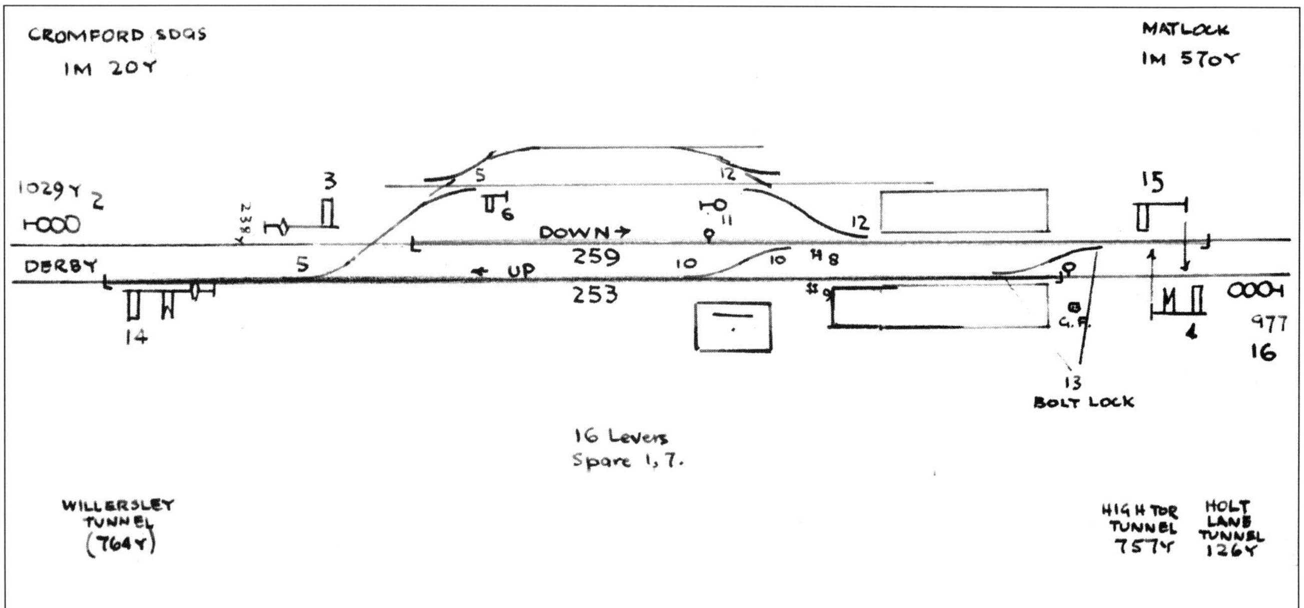

A diagram of the signal layout at Matlock Bath during its last few years. Charles would not have had the benefit of colour light distant signals when he worked there.

Charles retired from the railway on 20th September 1947. He was then just over 66½ years old. His wife Emma was 4 years older than him. They had had just over 3 years together in retirement when Emma died on 1st February 1951. Unfortunately, Charles survived her by just 2 months, as will be seen from the gravestone in St. Mark's Churchyard at Cromford. Their son Frank was buried in the same plot in 1998.

[Yvonne Daykin]

2. THE LOCAL RAILWAY SCENE AROUND CROMFORD 1912 TO 1917

The people named in this section are known to be / believed to have been local railwaymen, or people associated with local railway events. In some cases a certain amount of information is known about the individuals, but in others little has so far come to light. It has to be remembered, however, that much of the period was during wartime, and that employees in certain grades were moved from location to location to cover for men who had joined the Forces. Cromford, in fact, had 10 station porters during this period.

26.08.1912 A. Goodwin removed to Ambergate for Johnsons Sidings signalbox.

[possibly from Cromford Sidings].

23.09.1912 Started Matlock sewerage [works] against river.

[This would be the sewerage works at High Peak Junction (near Cromford L&NW Goods). Two parcels of land were purchased from the Midland Railway. The agreement to reserve the land was made between Matlock UDC and the Midland Railway on 1st March 1907, but the purchase agreement – for £116. 11s.0d – was not concluded until 17th March 1913.]

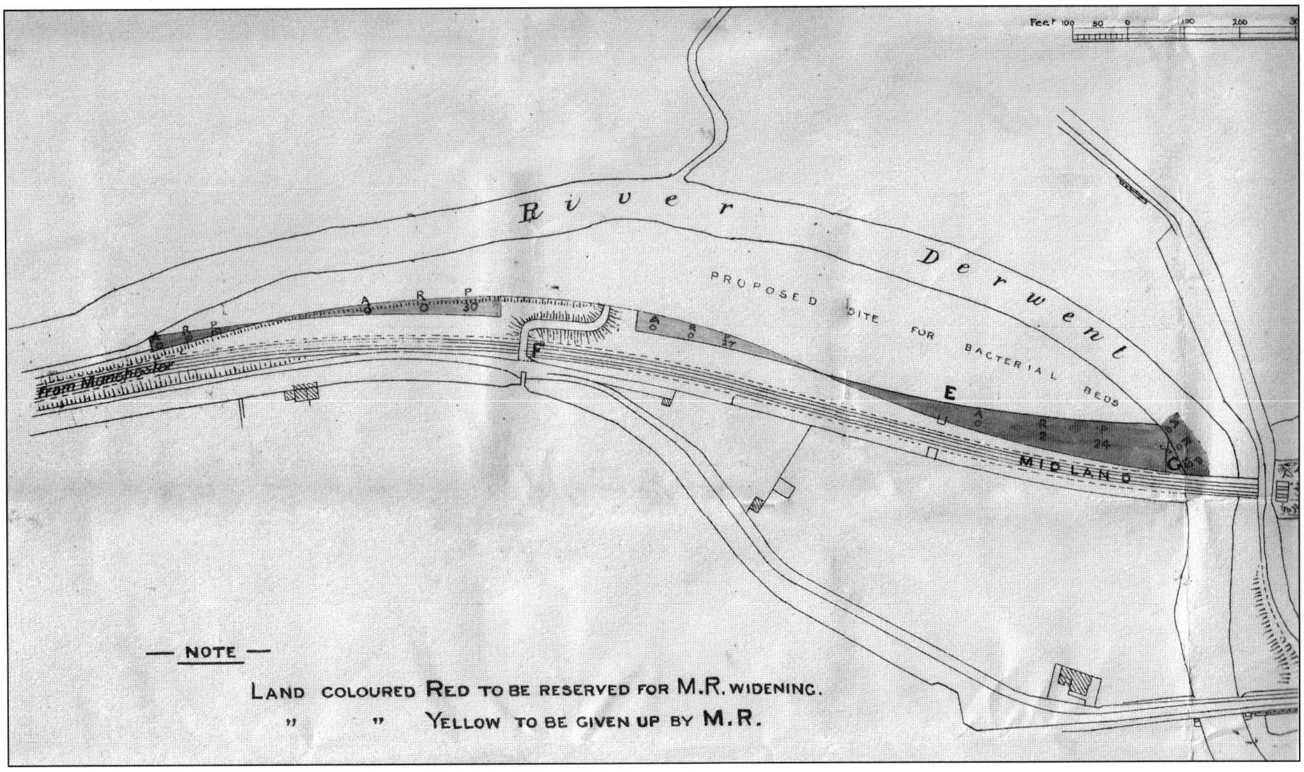

A diagram showing where the sewerage works were built and the land given up for this purpose (a lighter shade). Note the areas reserved by the Midland Railway for possible widening, particularly the one to the right near Leawood Tunnel. A similar area was reserved at the other end of the tunnel, indicating the possibility of a second, straighter, bore. The original alignment, which was altered in 1884, more-or-less followed the boundary line.

15.10.1912 R. Willan arrived Cromford [Sidings signal box]

[possibly replacement signalman for A. Goodwin – Roger Willan lived in Starkholmes].

18.11.1912 W. Boden knocked down in Willersley tunnel about 3.20pm. Engine No.3751. Died 19th November; buried 22nd November. [See Appendix "E"]

17.12.1912 G. Weaving arrived Cromford.

[It would appear that this was the third new Cromford Sidings signalman in a short period of time – first Charles in February 1911, then R. Willan in October 1912, and now G. Weaving.]

13.05.1913 G. Brown and W. Foster on nights watching for suffragettes.

[It is not known which department the men were from, but probably the Way & Works. It would be interesting to know which area they covered and how they policed it. It is understood that scout groups were also involved.]

30.07 1913 First class door open on 11.14am ex Derby. Engine No.492.

[It would appear that this occurred on Charles' shift. The 11.14am train ex Derby was the 10.47am Express from Nottingham to Manchester Central. After Derby its first booked stop was Matlock, so the train would have had to be stopped 'out of course' so that the guard could be advised to secure the door. It is likely that door was on its first catch rather than open in the true sense, otherwise it would surely have been noted before the train reached Cromford Sidings. It is not known whether Charles witnessed the position of the door and rang forward to Matlock Bath, or whether this was noticed at High Peak Junction, with Charles then stopping the train and contacting the guard.

No.492 was a Class 2 passenger engine with a 4-4-0 wheel arrangement which had been completely rebuilt during the previous year. It was withdrawn in December 1948. At the time of this incident it was allocated to Derby.]

08.1913 Trains passing Cromford Sidings in following years:

June 1906 – 844	July 1906 – 973
June 1910 – 844	July 1910 – 998
June 1913 – 876 (32 increase)	July 1913 – 998 (25 increase per week of 6 days)

[It is not recorded why Charles noted these statistics, or what the source was. One possibility is that it was in connection with a re-grading application, while the source could have been the box's train register book, in which every movement would have been recorded. It is almost certain, however, that the statistics relate to sample 6-day periods (Sundays excepted) during the particular months.

Appendix "F" records all the trains timed to pass Cromford Sidings signalbox during the period of the summer timetable for July, August and September 1914. The detail is taken from the Working Timetable for that period, supplemented by information from the Standard Excursion programme. While the figures for a sample week in July do not quite equate with those for the previous year – even taking into account 'Q' [runs as required] and suspended trains (which gives a total of 949), it has to be recognised that a number of special trains and light engines would also have run, particularly on the freight side.

Appendix "G" gives details of special excursion trains timed to pass the box during the 7-day period from 13th to 19th July 1914, while Appendix "H" shows the timetabled trains which were booked to call at Cromford station.]

Left: The signal box and sidings on 25th July 1964, with D97 passing on the 2.25pm from St. Pancras. Rowsley Sidings are now closed, so the three roads on the right would see little further use. [Author's collection / H.B. Priestley]

Right: More-or-less the same view in February 2007. In a few months time the leaves will have grown on the trees, making it even more difficult to make comparisons.

16.08.1913 J. Oldbury 9s.6d fine for riding bike without lights at Holmesford (sic) Cottage from Ambergate Flower Show [on this date]. Wirksworth court 26th August 1913.

[John Oldbury was a wagon examiner for the London & North Western Railway at High Peak Junction (Cromford Goods). He had covered that job from at least 1901. In the census of that year he was aged 23, a boarder – along with his wife – in the home of John Keightley of Scarthin. He later joined the Forces and was wounded in May 1915, but fortunately survived.]

19.08.1913 Matlock Bath Down distant [signal] light out. Closed box 2.44am, opened 3.22am.

[This signal was situated at the south end of Cromford station, just over 800 yards from the signalbox. As the nearest person at this time in the morning, Charles would have had to fill a spare signal lamp with oil, walk down the line to the station, change the lamp, and bring the empty one back with him.]

21.08.1913 Meeting at Matlock. Signalmen's movement. J. Wood chairman, Ambergate. J. Wood appointed delegate. The following branches were represented: Ambergate, Belper, Buxton, Cromford, Rowsley.

[James Wood was the secretary of the Ambergate branch of the Amalgamated Society of Railway Servants in 1910.]

28.08.1913 R. Willan's case dismissed. Mr Holmes fined 5s.0d, plus costs.

[As mentioned previously, Roger Willan was one of the signalmen in Cromford Sidings box. Both Willan and Holmes (a labourer from Riber) were charged with violent conduct relating to a fight outside the White Lion Inn at Starkholmes at 11.0pm on 8th August. A witness by the name of Fox said that Holmes was under the influence of drink and had struck Willan first. Holmes also had to pay 7s.6d costs.]

31.08.1913 National Union of Railwaymen Cromford Branch Meeting. Orphan Fund Parade arrangements: Mr Purslow and Mr J. Smith MCs; Mr W. Firth and Mr C. Burling Collectors; Mr H. Workman Secretary; E. Ashman ill.

[The NUR was constituted on 29th March 1913 by a combination of the Amalgamated Society of Railway Servants (formed 1872), the General Railway Workers' Union (1890) and the United Pointsmen's and Signalmen's Society (1880). The Cromford Branch was originally a branch of the ASRS. See Appendices "I" and "J". The Orphan Fund was established in 1875 to support the children of members who had died or been killed.]

14.09.1913 NUR Orphan Fund Parade – collected £13.9s.4d. Speakers E. Weightman of Ambergate and R. Moffatt of Birmingham. R. Buckle of Rowsley, Chairman, C.F. White etc. A. Gregory [given] 6d change making it £13.8.10d.

The breakdown of money collected was as follows [all would be members of the NUR]:

E. Ellis	£3. 9s. 5d	J.W. Spencer	12s. 7d
W. Gratton	£1. 4s. 9d	B. Staley	11s.11d
M. Willmott	£1. 2s. 8d	E. Taylor	9s. 7d
W. Firth	£1. 0s. 7d	A. Gregory	£1.10s. 1d
C. Burling	19s. 4d	Meeting boxes	2s. 7d
W. Spry	17s.10d	Meeting boxes	4s. 5d
M. Thompson	17s. 4d	Ward	6s. 2d
		Total	**£13. 9s. 4d**

[Those who can still add up in old currency will note the total is 1d more than the sum of the individual amounts!

Bob Buckle was the secretary of the Rowsley Branch of the NUR until July 1920.]

18.09.1913 J. Taylor removed from Matlock Bath to Tottenham as reliefman. [presumably a signalman].

19.09.1913 Both main lines blocked at Church Lane Crossing from 8.15pm until 11.45pm; wagons off the road. [See Appendix "K"]

07.10.1913 12 noon ex Manchester, engine No.1017. Axle broken against 142 milepost [train] run to High Peak Junction. Single line working from 2.0pm to 5.55pm. Mr Hewitt[8] Pilotman, damage to road, no-one injured.

[8] William Henry Hewitt was the Station Master at Whatstandwell from c.May 1911 to at least 1925.

[Cromford Sidings signalbox was at 142 miles 47 chains; High Peak Junction signalbox was at 141 miles 23 chains. Milepost 142 was adjacent to Cromford L&NW Goods at the bottom of Sheep Pasture incline. This could have caused quite a nasty accident, as the train had to cross the River Derwent, pass through the curved Lea Wood tunnel and cross the river again before reaching High Peak Junction.

The *High Peak News* of 18th October reported the incident under the heading *'Miraculous Escape of Train'* but appears to have got the story a little wrong. It stated that the crank axle of the engine broke when the train was passing through Cromford station at 60mph. This ripped into the permanent way and bent the rails, yet the train safely passed over the damaged portion. The damaged track prevented it being *'brought back'* (presumably to Cromford Sidings where there was a crossover) and it *'remained there four hours with its passengers in the carriages before it could proceed ... when the engine pulled up one of the wheels was off the rails'*.

[Engine 1017 was a 4-4-0 Compound, which was built in March 1906 as No.1012. It was renumbered 1017 in 1907 and 41017 after nationalisation in 1948. It was withdrawn in August 1950. At the time of this incident, the locomotive was allocated to Trafford Park (Manchester)].

Left: The position of milepost 142 taken in April 2007. In 1913 there would have been two lines, of course, whilst the section of the sewerage works at this point had probably not been started.

Right: The view from the other side of the overbridge. The Manchester-bound Midland Pullman passes Cromford Sidings' Down distant signal, having just emerged from Leawood Tunnel on 13th July 1961. The area to the left is quite open, having been retained for potential widening. In more recent times, however, most of this has been sold and utilised for an extension of the sewerage works. [H. Townley / C.M. & J.M Bentley collection]

08.10.1913 Mr Brown arrived Cromford as Station Master vice Mr Cooper going to Belle Vue on 13th October.

[Thomas Cooper had been the Station Master at Cromford from at least 1907. His replacement James Brown was initially reported in the *High Peak News* as *'someone from near London'*, but it was later revealed that he had been the Station Master at Buckden in Huntingdonshire.

Appendix "L" records what is known about the Station Masters at Cromford.]

09.10.1913 Signalman Worthing came to Whatstandwell. Refused to go to High Peak Junction. Went back to Longstone. Came from Monsal Dale.

[High Peak Junction signal box came under the control of the Station Master at Whatstandwell. Worthing presumably worked in Longstone signal box, but lived at Monsal Dale.]

11.10.1913 Signalman R. Smith came to High Peak Junction from Longstone vice E. Ashman to Whatstandwell Sidings, vice H. Bennett to Millers Dale Lime Sidings [see also next entry].

[An entry elsewhere in the notebook records that R. Smith joined the Midland Railway on 17th April 1905.

Longstone signal box closed at an unknown date between 1903 – when the original box was replaced – and 1920 – when it re-opened. Could the fact that two different signalmen from Longstone were involved in transfers to High Peak Junction indicate that the box closed around this time? A few days earlier – on 1st October 1913 – Longstone station had been renamed Great Longstone for Ashford.]

25.10.1913 E. Ashman took charge at Whatstandwell Sidings signalbox.
H. Bennett removed to Millers Dale Lime Sidings signalbox.

[In 1911 H. Bennett was the chairman of the union's Midland District Council. The annual accounts of the Cromford Branch of the ASRS for 31st December 1912 showed H. Bennett as an auditor from Whatstandwell, and E. Ashman as the branch secretary living at Robin Hood, Whatstandwell.]

Left: High Peak Junction signal box on 4th March 1967, the last day of operation on the lower end of the Cromford & High Peak line and for local passenger services between Derby and Manchester. The box continued in use until 29th October of the same year. [M.A. King]

Right: Saltley 8F No.48331 passes Whatstandwell Sidings signalbox with an Up mixed goods on 24th May 1952. The Down platform of the original Whatstandwell Bridge station, which closed on 11th November 1894, can be seen in the centre foreground. [E.R. Morten]

29.10.1913 J. Essex took charge at Matlock Bath. [presumably a signalman]

01.11.1913 Signal Fitter F. Eley found dead south end of Dove Holes Tunnel at 3.0am. [see Appendix "M"]

01.11.1913 6.40pm goods train divided between Matlock and Darley Dale. 6.30pm express ex London delayed.

[This was a Saturday evening. The goods train would have been the 6.40pm Mineral from Derby Station to Rowsley, which was due to recess in Cromford Sidings from 8.12pm to 8.53pm, and pass Matlock just after 9.0pm. The London to Manchester express was scheduled to pass through Matlock around 9.30pm.

No mention of the incident has been found in local papers, so presumably it was of a minor nature, or did not affect passenger trains which called at stations in the Matlock area.]

13.11.1913 Signalmen's meeting at Grouse Hotel, Darley Dale. Branches involved – Ambergate, Rowsley, Belper and Cromford.

17.11.1913 New Station Porter vice Hill arrived.

24.11.1913 Porter Hill removed to Glapwell.

[No name given. Possibly J. Pickering (see 21.02.1914) or J.P. Burrows (see 02.12.1914).]

26.11.1913 Reliefman vice Sturgeon arrived from London. [presumably covered signalling duties.]

01.12.1913 Porter J. Varty removed from Whatstandwell to Kelston as Porter in Charge.

[Kelston for Saltford – to be precise – was situated near Bath on land owned by Colonel Inigo Jones of Kelston Park, who had the power to stop any train providing that he gave 24 hours notice. The station was also unusual in that it had no road access, just a path across the fields.]

08.12.1913 King and Queen arrived Rowsley. Returned 13th December to London.

[This was the first visit to Chatsworth by King George V since he became King. The occasion was notable in that the practice of issuing card passes to selected people to view the Royal Party on the platform at Rowsley station was suspended, due to rumours that a band of suffragettes were expected to cause trouble.]

Left: When Porter Hill moved to Glapwell in November 1913 he would have found a scene somewhat different from that at Cromford. The station was on a single line with just 3 passenger trains each way a day, plus 3 additional ones on Saturdays. On the other hand, as can be seen in this photograph, there was plenty of activity connected with the adjacent colliery.

Right: Kelston for Saltford station at the turn of the 20th century. Although rather remote, 7 Up (Bristol direction) and 9 Down trains were booked to call at the station when Porter Varty moved there. Trains did not call on Sundays.

10.12.1913 Queen's visit to Derby via Matlock, Cromford, and Belper. [by motor car]

16.12.1913 Ganger Smith killed in Milford tunnel. [see Appendix "N"]

17.12.1913 G. Weaving [signalman, Cromford] married at Bakewell.

24.12.1913 Both main lines blocked between Monsal Dale and Longstone about 4.40am. Freight train divided, rear portion ran into first portion.

[According to the *High Peak News* the incident actually occurred about 30 yards inside Headstone Tunnel and completely disorganised holiday traffic. Trains were diverted via the Dore & Chinley line, while a service of local passenger trains operated on either side of the blockage. The tunnel was apparently full of debris for some distance, but this was cleared and the line opened by the evening.]

LMS Compound No.1050 is seen here passing over Monsal Dale viaduct having just left Headstone Tunnel with a northbound express. The engine entered service in March 1924. It looks to be in pristine condition, which indicates that the photo was taken around that time. The two portions of the divided train met 30 yards inside Headstone tunnel in the mishap on Christmas Eve 1913, which indicates that a number of the wagons in the rear portion would have come to rest on the viaduct.

[M.L. Knighton collection]

26.12.1913 (and 27.12.1913) Reliefman W. Hart vice Willan.

[Hart was covering for two day's leave. See also 23.01.1915 and Section 1 – 06.09.1915.

In those days, men who covered sickness and holiday relief at signalboxes often relieved Station Masters and other supervisory grades. Separate relief posts for signalmen and Station Masters do not appear to have been introduced until the time of the 1920 agreements.]

27.12.1913 NUR Orphan Fund collection at Cromford by W. Firth and C. Burling. £2.12.6d paid to E. Ashman.

[An earlier note stated that W. Firth went into Derby Infirmary from 19th to 22nd December, so he did well to be involved in such a collection – or did Charles do most of the work on this occasion?]

29.12.1913 Yates of Crich Carr injured in Clay Cross Tunnel, taken to Chesterfield Hospital.

[The *Derbyshire Times* makes brief mention of this incident. Yates (no forename is given) was a bricklayer from Ambergate, who was engaged in carrying out emergency repairs in the tunnel. He was knocked down by the 3.40pm express from Derby to Sheffield and was conveyed to Chesterfield Hospital on a light engine. It was found that he was suffering from shock and a fractured arm.]

30.12.1913 Reliefman B. Wilson went to Longstone as Station Master.

[Bernard Wilson was still the Station Master at Great Longstone in January 1922, but had been replaced by 1925.]

Great Longstone for Ashford station looking north in Midland Railway days. It is quite possible that one of the men on the platform is Station Master Bernard Wilson. Note the signal box, which was probably only open on an as required basis at this time. See entries in October 1913 re transfer of signalmen.

[M.L. Knighton collection]

01.01.1914 Total number of members of the Cromford & District branch of the NUR = 89. [See Appendix "I"]

01.1914 NUR : Election of delegates to the AGM Group No. 34

Amos, R. – 2 Cromford
Burford, W. – Buxton
Carey, W. – Belper and Duffield
Drinkwater, G.T. – New Mills
Varney, S.W. – 3 Ripley
Waterson A.E. – 1 Derby No.2

R. Amos should be A. Rowland[9]. [signalman High Peak Junction]

[These would be the representatives from the individual branches. It is not known what the figure 1, 2 and 3 are preceding three of the branch names.]

17.01.1914 G. Weaving [signalman Cromford Sidings] asked to accept Rowsley Sidings box. [declined?]

01.02.1914 Meeting at Middleton to discuss opening of new branch of the NUR at that location.

[The *Railway Review*[10], which reported regularly on new branches, makes no reference to one having been formed at Middleton at this time. However, a new branch at Matlock was formed at the end of October of the following year.]

The 'Hanger On' makes sure that everything is OK as three vehicles – two ex-L&NWR water tenders and a common user wagon – start their descent of Middleton incline on an unspecified occasion in the 1950s. Had a branch of the NUR been formed at Middleton it would have mainly consisted of men who worked on the Cromford & High Peak line.

[R. Eckersley]

[9] His full name was Amos Rowland. The NUR had obviously transposed the surename and forename!

[10] The weekly newspaper of the ASRS / NUR.

03.02.1914 Midland Railway signalmen's meeting at Ambergate to hear delegate of Conciliation Board No.2.

05.02.1914 Midland Railway signalmen's meeting at Millers Dale, to hear results of Conciliation Board No.2 re signalmen's movement. Voting for accepting Company's offer – 10 for; 9 against.

10.02.1914 Conciliation Board No. 2 meeting at Derby. [See Appendix "C"]

15.02.1914 J.H. Bond joined NUR – Scale C.

[not known who this person was, or why he was mentioned specifically]

21.02.1914 Porter Mr J. Pickering badly burnt at Cromford station. Taken to Derby Infirmary 7.11pm train, died 11.45pm. Buried 25th February. Attended funeral. Bearers: A. Burdett, G. Weaving, J. Roe, C. Burling, H. Allen, J. Vearnals.

26.02.1914 Inquest re Porter Pickering at Derby. Cleaning floor with naptha. Accidental death. [see Appendix "O"]

28.03.1914 Meeting at Matlock for whist drive and dance for 7th May 1914.

[This particular entry tells us little, but from other records it is almost certain that this related to an NUR Orphans Fund event – see entry for 01.04.1914]

30.03.1914 G. Prince came to Cromford from Darley Dale vice Pickering.

01.04.1914 Messrs Ashman, Burdett, Smith and Burling went to see manager re whist drive and dance.

[See entry for 28.03.1914. All were members of the NUR Cromford Branch. The venue was probably the Assembly Rooms.]

12.04.1914 Derby & District Banner Fund. 1s.0d returned to H. Workman.

[This was presumably a fund for providing banners for NUR parades. H. Workman was one of the officials of the Cromford & District Branch. It is shown elsewhere in the notebook that the secretary of the Banner Fund around this time was Mr F. Humphries, 9 Hardwick Street, Osmaston Road, Derby.]

An NUR Derby & District banner for use in Orphan Fund parades. Some branches had their own banners, but others hired them from the larger branches. The *Railway Review* contained a section each week, which was devoted to the hiring of banners for such events.

14.05.1914 Signalman's meeting at Hurt Arms Hotel, Ambergate. The next one to be held at Bakewell 12 weeks from this date.

31.05.1914 Parade at Wirksworth and Middleton in aid of NUR Orphan Fund. Mr Chorlton and Mr C.F. White speakers. Collection £6.7s.0d.

07.06.1914 First meeting of the Cromford & District branch of the NUR held at Greyhound Hotel reading room.

[Meetings were previously held in the Rutland Arms Hotel at Masson, but the room had become too small to accommodate the expanding membership.]

The Rutland Arms hotel is the large building at the end of the row of houses in this photograph from around the First World War period. The entrance to Masson Mill was on the right of the photograph opposite the hotel. All of the buildings were demolished in a road widening scheme in the early 1970s, while Masson Mill – then one of the biggest places of employment in the district – is now a shopping complex. Nowadays, it is hard to believe that there was room for such buildings. [K. Smith collection]

10.08.1914 G. Prince [station porter] called up for the Forces. Went to Derby this day by 12.30pm train.

[Prince – Midland Railway records show his initials as G.H. – was one of the first to join the Forces, war having only been declared on 4th August. It is believed that he was around 20 years of age.]

29.08.1914 Watch guessing competition on behalf of Byard of Derby. 2d worth. Results in *Derby Telegraph*, *Daily Citizen* and *Railway Review*.

[Would appear to be a fund raising event – possibly organised by the NUR.]

29.08.1914 Troop train arrived at Cromford Sidings Engine No.3713.

[This would no doubt have been the empty stock from a troop train to a local destination rather than a train with passengers, equipment and animals.

The locomotive was built in 1901 as No.2684, renumbered 3713 in 1907 and withdrawn from service in June 1930. It was allocated to Bristol at this time, but had a new boiler fitted in Derby Works during 1914, so may have been used on 'running in' duties.]

31.08.1914 Porter W. Saunders arrived Cromford vice Prince on active service.

07.09.1914 29 [Forces] recruits from Cromford went to Derby. 21 passed including C. Parker and G. Finch from Matlock Bath station.

02.12.1914 J.P. Burrows joined R.A.M.C. Went to Leeds 5th December 1914.

[Burrows worked at Cromford station – see entry below]

14.12.1914 J. Roe vice Burrows at Station. [presumably a reliefman – see 21.12.1914]

18.12.1914 Both main lines blocked at High Peak Junction. Wagon of coal off road at crossover road. Signalman A. Rowland on duty.

Later entry: Wingfield Manor wagon 592 arrived damaged on the 1.5pm freight Rowsley to Ambergate. Came off road while detaching it into Down siding at crossover road, both lines blocked. Train arrived 1.25pm; wagon off road 1.39pm; down line clear 2.23pm; single line working 2.36pm. Ordinary working resumed 4.50pm, Engine No.3271 Guard. Elliott of Rowsley. Breakdown vans arrived 2.23pm; departed 4.8pm. Single working between High Peak Jn and Matlock Bath. Mr Hewitt [Station Master, Whatstandwell] pilotman.

[Engine No.3271 was allocated to Buxton shed at this time; Rowsley was a sub-shed of Buxton until 1935. The guard was presumably 'Photo Joe' Elliott, who originated from Bonsall and took many evocative photographs of both railway and village scenes at Rowsley.]

An atmospheric view of 1873 Class 0-6-0 No.1946 and staff taken at Rowsley shed by 'Photo Joe' Elliott around the turn of the 20th century. The engine was renumbered 3273 in 1907. Sister engine 3271 was in charge of the train that derailed at High Peak Junction in the account on the previous page.

20.12.1914 12.1am ex Manchester delayed between Cromford and Whatstandwell.

[no reason is given for this delay – nothing mentioned in local papers]

21.12.1914 A. Parker started at Cromford Station as porter vice J.P. Burrows.

12.1914 Inspector Dale W & W [Way & Works Dept.] left Matlock Bath for Ashchurch. Inspector Ledbetter W & W arrived Matlock Bath from Carlisle vice Dale removed.

[Ganger S. Bateman of Cromford presented William Dale with a *'purse of gold'* at Hodgkinson's Hotel. Matlock Bath, on Saturday 2nd January 1915. The edition of the *High Peak News* issued on the same date stated that Ledbetter was actually from Settle.]

08.01.1915 J. Daniels [signalman Whatstandwell] been offered a removal to Bitton as signalman. [see also 19.04.1915]

[Bitton is near Bath. Perhaps Daniels had requested a transfer to that part of the country.]

11.01.1915 Signalman Workman on duty 3 days 11th, 12th and 13th January.

[Another entry where Charles would have known the full reason, but where it leaves the reader nowadays to speculate on what might have happened. The underlining was made by Charles.]

16.01.1915 G. Weaving asked to accept Rowsley sidings box. Refused.

23.01.1915 to 25.01.1915 Reliefmen Hart & Woodcroft vice Mr Brown [Station Master].

[Hart has been mentioned previously as relieving signalmen. Joseph Lionel Woodcroft is recorded as covering duties at Matlock station when Station Master Clarke died at the end of March 1911, and was relieving at Darley Dale station when Donald Preece was killed on 19th March 1915. – see Appendix "P"]

01.02.1915 The Reserve of the Notts & Derbyshire Regiment removed Buxton to Aldershot and Seaford 1st and 2nd February; Luton 3rd February.

12.02.1915 8 officers and 350 men from Aldershot arrived Matlock Bath (Army Service Corps).

[Although not specifically mentioned, this move and subsequent ones recorded in the notebook, would have been by rail. The movements themselves do not appear to have been reported in the local press – perhaps understandably, as there was a war in progress. However, comments on their billeting in the district were made from time to time. In fact, the businessmen of Matlock Bath welcomed the troops as they replaced – from a spending point of view – the excursionists that no longer visited the district due to the withdrawal of such facilities by rail.]

20.02.1915 Mr Brown [Station Master] off ill.

22.02.1915 187 officers and men and 42 horses from Woolwich arrived Matlock Bath.

28.02.1915 W. Saunders [porter at Cromford station] off ill.

01.03.1915 W. Firth went to Leeds to join R.A.M.C. [presumably the person previously mentioned as a collector for the NUR at Orphan Fund events.]

01.03.1915 15 officers and 1,100 men arrived Matlock.

02.03.1915 130 officers and men arrived Matlock.

04.03.1915 7th Battalion West Yorkshire 24 officers and 740 men [arrived Matlock?]

04.03.1915 No.2 company A.S.C. 6 officers and 120 men [arrived Matlock?]

05.03.1915 2nd & 5th West Yorkshire 22 officers and 530 men arrived Matlock Bath.

06.03.1915 Fever broken out amongst troops at Matlock Bath. [Does not appear to have been reported in the local papers – would have been bad publicity.]

The railways saw vast numbers of troop movements during the war. Unfortunately, no photographs are known of those recorded in Charles' notebook, but the scenes outside the stations would almost certainly have been similar to this one taken at Buxton during the same period. Buxton had two stations side by side – one owned by the L&NWR, on the left, and the other by the Midland Railway, on the right. Because the exits from both stations led to the same assembling area, it is not certain which one they had used. Their arrival obviously created interest from the local inhabitants, even though it was clearly a rainy day.

08.03.1915 9 officers, 300 men and 20 horses arrived Darley Dale.

15.03.1915 A. Parker [porter, Cromford Station] off ill.

16.03.1915 23 officers and 704 men arrived Darley Dale.

18.03.1915 C. Parker home on furlough. [based at Matlock Bath – see 07.09.1914.]

19.03.1915 Lad aged 14 killed at Darley Dale by 1.25pm passenger train ex Buxton. [see Appendix "P"]

05.04.1915 E. Porter arrived Whatstandwell vice J. Daniels.

08.04.1915 West Yorkshire men moved from Matlock Bath to Doncaster. Also on following day.

19.04.1915 J. Daniels removed to Bitton from Whatstandwell. [Bitton was the next station to Kelston to where Whatstandwell Porter J. Varty moved in December 1913.]

A Bath-bound train entering Bitton station c.1910. The signalbox is in the left background.

05.1915 Private G. Thompson 6th Notts & Derby killed in action.

[George Thompson was a shunter based at Matlock, who lived in Upper Hackney. According to other records he died on 12th May. George's brother Matthew was a porter at Matlock station.]

05.06.1915 Mr Sims of Whatstandwell killed on line by 8.55am ex Manchester. [see Appendix "Q"]

06.06.1915 Open meeting of the Cromford and District branch of the N.U.R. Speaker Mr Halls of Nottingham.

13.06.1915 Troops removed from Darley Dale to Masham. A.S.C.

14.06.1915 A. Goodwin [signalman Johnson's Sidings, Ambergate – see 26.08.1912] reported himself at Matlock re joining the army. Refused had not got permit.

21.06.1915 Shunter J. Ward of Matlock ran into Mr S. Bateman while riding a bicycle down Cromford Hill. Died 22nd June. Buried 25th June 1915 at Wirksworth. Inquest accidental death. [see Appendix "R"]

07.07.1915 Porter J. Wood arrived Cromford station vice W. Saunders removed to Buxton 9th August 1915.

[It would appear that J. Wood needed quite a bit of training – probably a new recruit.]

13.09.1915 Mr Brown [Station Master] on leave for 12 days.

24.10.1915 G. Brown, E. Bateman, E. Higton, and A Parker [porter at Cromford station] joined the NUR.

10.1915 [Not mentioned in Charles' notebook was the formation of a branch of the NUR at Matlock. 26 men were transferred from the Cromford & District branch. [see Appendix "I"]

11.1915 52 single men, 73 married in W & W Department between 18 and 40 years old.

[Presumably men who could be 'called up'.]

06.11.1915 G. Weaving [signalman Cromford Sidings] failed to pass Doctor for Army Reserve. [see also 09.1916]

12.11.1915 E. Ashman and R. Smith passed Doctor for Army Reserve for active service at home and abroad.

[This took place on the same day that Charles visited the Army doctor (see entry in Section 1). E. Ashman was a signalman at Whatstandwell; R Smith was a signalman at High Peak Junction.]

15.11.1915 A. Rowland and E. Porter passed for Army Reserve.

[A. Rowland was a signalman at High Peak Junction; E. Porter was a signalman at Whatstandwell.]

19.11.1915 R. Willan and A. Goodwin passed Doctor for Army Reserve B.

[R. Willan was a signalman at Cromford Sidings; A Goodwin was a signalman at Johnson's Sidings in 1912.]

10.12.1915 A. Goodwin removed. [To Army?]

? . 12.1915 Carriage door open on the 9.15pm express Derby to Manchester. R. Willan reported it. (on duty 2pm to 10pm). [Appears to have been working an 8 hour shift rather than the 10 hour shifts previously referred to. Perhaps the war had forced a change.]

16.01.1916 Mr A. Rowland [signalman High Peak Junction] transferred to the Ambergate branch of the NUR. [possibly transferred to a signalbox in the Ambergate area].

Compound No.1024 pulls away from the curve at Ambergate station and passes the West Junction signal box with a Manchester-bound express c.1910.

26.02.1916 Ganger H. Spencer died of fatty degeneration of the heart. Buried 29th February at Bonsall Church Yard.

14.03.1916 Mr Mason of Matlock Bath killed at Ambergate Station. Inquest accidental death. [see Appendix "S"]

27.04.1916 12 troop specials to Liverpool for Ireland. [A reaction to rebellion in Dublin from 24th to 26th April.]

07.1916 Rowsley North Jn signal box vacancy. £1.10.0d, with bonus £1.15.0d 1st week; £2.1.7d, with bonus £2.6.7d 2nd week; £1.17.2d, with bonus £2.2.2d 3rd week. [Appears to have been in Class 8 – see Appendix "C"]

Compound No.1032 passes Rowsley North Junction signal box with a Down excursion in LMS days. Charles would no doubt have worked here during his time as a relief signalman at Rowsley between 1927 and 1933.

11.07.1916 W. Eaden at Derby Station A Box. [NUR official?]

J. Pullen removed from Ambergate to Melbourne Junction.

18.07.1916 Woman from Ilkeston killed at Ambergate station. [see Appendix "S"]

09.1916 G. Weaving at Derby. Failed for the Army with his heart. [see also 06.11.1915]

10.09.1916 [NUR] Parade at Cromford, Matlock Bath and Matlock. Mr Chorlton speaker at open meeting. £10.0.0d collected, expenses £5.0.0d.

26.09.1916 A. Parker [porter, Cromford Station] off ill to 23rd October. J. Hodgson vice Parker.

23.04.1917 Mr Coates commenced work at Cromford station as porter vice Wood.

25.04.1917 J. Wood passed for Army in Class A.

02.05.1917 W. Gregory started at Cromford station.

19.06.1917 J. Wood of Cromford, H. Allen, M.Thompson Wright of Matlock, also A. Parker joined Army. [Not all railway employees? – Wood and Parker were the two porters at Cromford station.]

And this is where the main notebook finishes. There are a few later entries for 1917, but these relate solely to conditions of service and payment. Had Charles added further information about local events in 1917, he would have told us about the two local men who lost their lives in Dove Holes Tunnel on the morning of Sunday 8th September – 19 year old Enos Mycroft of Starkholmes and 18 year old Arnold Powndall of Bonsall – and of painter George Cooper of Darley Dale falling from scaffolding on one of the viaducts at Millers Dale on Sunday 25th November – but one wonders why he did not mention the whist drive and dance in aid of the *'Railway Servants Widows and Orphans'* held in the Assembly Rooms at Matlock on the evening of Thursday 8th March. This was reported as a *'great success'* with *'26 tables of whist players and a large number of dancers'*, though modesty may have prevented him repeating the last sentence of the *High Peak News* report, which read *'Mr Charles Burling is to be congratulated on his success as secretary and promoter of the event'*. This gentleman brought up in rural Cambridgeshire, who came to Cromford at the beginning of 1911, was now an active and well-regarded figure in the area.

3. GENERAL CIRCULARS, NOTICES AND OTHER MISCELLANEOUS INFORMATION 1912 TO 1917

24.10.1913 Circular received this day, as follows:

General Supts. Office, Derby, May 3rd 1913 SD3/150.

Annual leave of absence. There is no objection to men in the same grade exchanging dates fixed for their holidays provided they mutually agree to do so. It should be understood however that the current year's scheduled dates will be taken as the basis when dates for subsequent holidays are being arranged.

General Supt.

24.10.1913 [The following is significant in that it sets out the signalmen's demands, which ultimately led to the agreement of 13th February 1914 – see Appendix "C". As will be seen, however, not all of these demands were conceded. For examples, most men just received 1s.0d per week rise, while the 8-hour day was not introduced until 1st February 1919.]

Signalmen's Programme signed October 24th 1913

To: Cecil W. Paget Esq
General Superintendent
Midland Railway
Derby

Sir,

In accordance with Clause 2 of the Conciliation scheme 1911 and on behalf of the following grades, Foreman signalmen, Signalmen, Porter Signalmen, Relief Signalmen and Train Recorders in the employ of the Midland Railway Co., the respective Committees of the Furness and Midland Joint Line, Otley and Ilkley Joint Line, Ashby & Nuneaton Joint Line, Great Central and Mid Joint Line, Tottenham & Hampstead Joint Line, Tottenham & Forest Gate Joint Railway, Halesowen Joint Railway, Clifton Extension Joint Railway and other Joint Railway or Joint Stations, the employees of which are grouped under the Midland Conciliation Board No. 2 being of opinion that the time has arrived for a revision of our conditions of employment. We beg to submit the following application and ask that the undermentioned deputation be received by the Directors to consider the same.

[signed] *Beswick, Cindery, Harris, Turner, Wood, Green.* [see page 33]

Presented to the Company on 5th November 1913.

Signalman's Programme 1913

Hours

That 8 hours constitute the standard day for all men coming under Conciliation Board 2. But should the Company desire a man to sign on or off duty at any place other than where his daily work is performed such extra service to be paid for on overtime basis.

Wages

A. That all men coming under Conciliation Board 2 receive an immediate advance of 4/- per week providing that in no case must a man be paid less than 30/- per week rate.

B. That no alteration be made in the rate of pay of any post during the period covered by the settlement except with the consent of the Conciliation Board.

C. That every man performing the duties of signalman including the present assistant signalmen and porter signalman shall receive the rate of pay of the signalman at that post.

That the rate of pay of the men compelled to live in the Swansea Valley district be 3/- per week higher than the same class of post in other parts except London, owing to the higher rents and costs of living.

Guaranteed week

That all men coming under Conciliation Board 2 be guaranteed a week's wage independent of Sunday duty.

Minimum day

That each time a man comes on duty he shall receive not less than one day's pay.

Promotion

That all vacancies be advertised in the weekly notice and the position be granted to the person who is the senior applicant from whatever part of the parent or joint line he may come.

This settlement shall apply continuously until varied, superseded or nullified by agreement between the Company and representatives of the employees or between the Company and the Executive Council of the NUR in accordance with any machinery that may exist for the purpose at the time of its termination.

Deputation

J.H. Cooper, Leicester (Chairman)
C.H. Green, Normanton (Secretary)
J. Cindery, Birmingham
J.C. Turner, Irchester
E.H. Beswick, Dore & Totley
H. Harris, Glais
J. Wood, Ambergate.

(69% of signalmen signed)

21.11.1913 *Midland Railway Co Signalmen's programme*

Deputation at Derby. Company refused to discuss any of the points in the programme. Referred to Conciliation Boards No. 2.

31.12.1913 NUR membership 267,611 of whom 263,432 are in present service of the Railways.

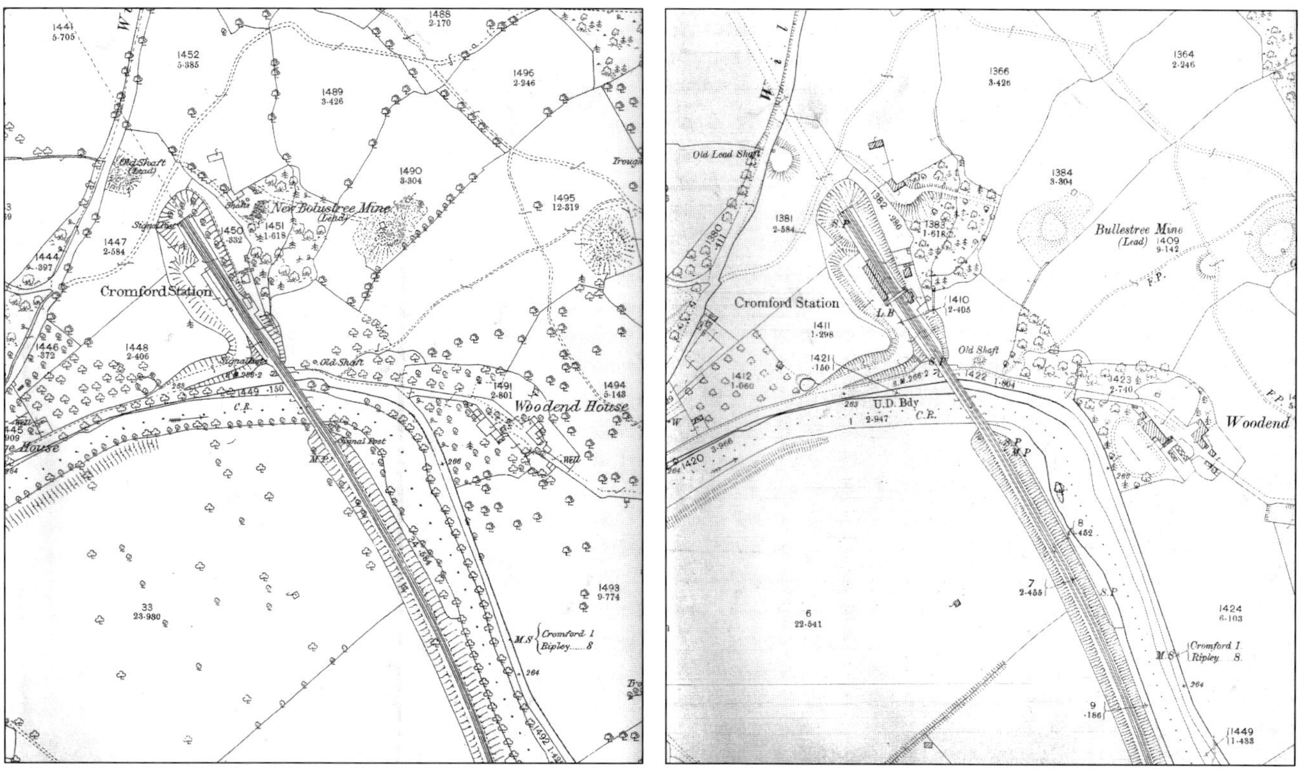

Extracts from the 25" OS maps for 1880 and 1898. Note that there is no footbridge at the station on the former. This was erected in 1885.

01.1914 Letter received as follows:

Split turn working Coaching Department Conciliation Board No. 4.

Referring to the above subject and I am pleased to inform you that on Jan 8th 1914 we were successful in getting the Independent Chairman to rule that the split turn system, as it applies to all men coming under Board No.4 must cease from that date Jan 8th or the men must be paid for the gross hours worked. Of course if the split turns are worked on Sundays the men must be paid for the gross hours at the rate of time and a quarter.

J. T. White.

[Conciliation Board No.4 covered passenger guards, station porters and others involved in the working of passenger trains.]

14.02.1914 The total [route]mileages worked by the following companies:

L&NW 1975½; Midland 1744.

02.04.1914 Meeting in London of the Railway Managers and the NUR

Managers:
Sir Guy Grant MR
Mr H.A. Walker L&SWR
Mr F. Potter GWR
Sir Sam Fay GCR
Sir R Turnbill and Mr G. Calthorp L&NWR
Mr Jackson NBR
Mr Beesley Taff Vale

NUR:
Mr A. Bellamy (President)
Mr J.E. Williams and Mr J.H. Thomas MP (Secretarys)
Mr Cramp
Mr Cuthbert
Mr Charles (EC)
Mr W. Hudson MP;

Secretary Mr W. Clower of the MR.

12.1914 NUR new members for 1914 – 68,414

05.02.1915 Notice from Midland Railway to staff stating that the company are desirous that none of their staff join the Home Defence Corps without their sanction.

[This was the time that many Home Guard units were being formed. On 27th February the *High Peak News* reported that the Cromford unit had over 30 people in training. Earlier in the month – on 6th February – it had reported on the formation of the Rowsley Home Guards, a village where around half the houses were occupied by railwaymen. It would appear that concern was expressed about the Midland's stance and on 26th June – relating specifically to the Rowsley Home Guard – the paper reported that a letter had been received from the Midland Railway stating that it had no objection to men joining the Home Guards providing that the Company had first call on their services. Many of the Rowsley men became expert riflemen, winning several competitions against other units and depots on the Midland system.]

06.02.1915 The General Managers of several railways met the Executive Committees of the NUR and ASLEF to discuss an advance of wages. Meeting adjourned.

28.09.1915 NUR Executive Committee met the General Managers of the railways – also on 1st October 1915.

05.04.1917 Privilege tickets stopped from 5th to 10th April. Order cancelled 4th April 1917.

[It is assumed that the notice suspending the facility was issued prior to 4th April, otherwise the cancellation would have appeared before the original notice! The original plan was to withdraw the facility over the Easter period – Easter Sunday was 8th April.]

10.06.1917 Midland Railway Conciliation Board No. 2.

J.C. Turner Men's Representative. Copy:

Dear Sir & Bros,

Basis of promotion of signalmen.

A case having arisen which necessitated some understanding as to what was the actual basis of promotion of signalmen. Our Secretary took up with the Company on the matter. He has since had an opportunity of discussing the point of difference with Mr Clower who has seen the Company's expert respecting the practice. He now informs me that Signalmen are promoted on the basis of their length of service in any particular class of signal box. He also states the question of the hours by applicant does not enter into the factors determining the promotion. Some years ago we were informed of an opposite view and maybe I have written you at some time on those lines. I am therefore now writing to advise you of the real position.

Yours faithfully, J.C. Turner.

To Secretary NUR, Cromford Branch.

Received 29th July 1917.

No. 58

Class 4 Freight Engine

11.58am to 7.30PM (SX)

	arr.	dep.
	a.m.	a.m.
Rowsley M.P.D.	....	11.58LE.SX
	P.M.	P.M.
Rowsley Up Sdgs	....	12.23 SX
Darley Dale	12.33	1. 8 SX
Matlock	1.17	2. 5 SX
A-Matlock Bath	2.12	2.58LE.SX
Cromford Sdgs	3. 3	3. 5LE.SX
B-Matlock Bath	3.10	3.33 SX
C-Matlock	3.40	6.55 SX
Rowsley Sth	7.20	7.25 SX
Rowsley Sdgs	7.30	.... SX
Rowsley M.P.D.	7.35	....

A-Pick up full water can for Cromford Sidings.
B-Set down empty water can from Cromford Sidings.
C-Also attach parcels van rear 5. 5PM Buxton to Derby.

Left: Cromford Sidings, like many signal boxes, did not have running water. It was also not adjacent to any building with such facilities. It was therefore necessary for water to be brought to the box in cans. As will be seen from this extract from the Derby area trip notice for September 1962, the water was brought from Matlock Bath by an engine that shunted the goods yard. The engine crew would exchange full and empty cans with the signalman and then use the crossover to return to Matlock Bath. There was also a similar trip on a Saturday, but this was in the morning. In this case, the engine was at Cromford Sidings from 9.47am to 10.14pm, so it was presumably 'put inside' for other trains to pass.

Below: A somewhat unusual view of Sheep Pasture incline, possibly taken from the Lea side of the River Derwent. The offices and workshop at Cromford Goods L&NWR are hidden behind the bushes on the right, but the high signal at the bottom on the incline is partly visible. To its left can be seen Cromford Sidings' Down distant signal. The white spot on the face indicates that the photo was taken prior to 1906. The large building in the centre included the C&HP Agent's House.

APPENDIX "A"
SIGNALLING ARRANGEMENTS AND DEVELOPMENTS AT CROMFORD

As this appendix will be read by people who may not be aware of the intricacies of railway signalling, it is perhaps best to write a few words about the general arrangements.

Main lines were split into block sections, access to and egress from adjacent sections being controlled from signal boxes. Under normal circumstances, a signalbox would have three main line signals in each direction:

– a distant or caution signal positioned some way from the box; if this was in the 'off' position[1], then the road would be clear to the next section. If it was in the 'on' position, then the driver had to be prepared to stop at the next (home) signal. If the braking distance was considered insufficient for the driver to stop his train at the home signal, then a second (outer) distant signal would be positioned a few hundred yards to the rear.

– a home or stop signal, normally situated a few yards before the signal box (though not initially in one direction at Cromford Sidings). If this was in the 'on' position, then the driver had to stop.

– a starting signal in advance of the signal box, which when pulled off allowed access into the next section. Again, if this was in the 'on' position then the driver had to stop. It was common practice after stopping a train at a home signal to let it move forward to the starting signal – probably with verbal instruction – to await the forward section to clear.

To complicate matters, in earlier years signals were sometimes provided at stations which were not block posts to enable trains calling there to be protected. This applied at Cromford until 1911. The normal practice was to have a distant and home signal in the rear of the station on each line. These signals were normally in the 'off' position, but when a train stopped at the station one of the staff would place them to the 'on' position using turnover levers located on the platform. After the train had departed the signals would be put back to the 'off' position after a prescribed period of time.

As mentioned elsewhere, Cromford Sidings signal box was opened on 1st September 1890. Prior to that time, the two adjacent signal boxes were at Matlock Bath station (see page 18) and High Peak Junction – where there was a connection with the Cromford & High Peak line (see page 23).

However, 'protection' signals for trains at Cromford station were installed several years earlier, possibly from 1874 when the building on the Down (Matlock direction) platform was erected, but certainly by 1880 as signal posts are shown on the 25" ordnance survey maps produced in that year (see page 33). In fact around Cromford station there was an abundance of signals, some due to the presence of Willersley tunnel. Illustrated opposite top is an extract from an undated 2-chain plan of the area, probably prepared in the early part of the 20th century, but still more-or-less covering the situation in 1880.

In the Down direction, the sequence of signals was:

Cromford station's distant – not on this particular diagram, but situated along the lower part of the Meadows [see 1880 OS map opposite]

Cromford station's home and Matlock Bath's outer distant on one post, situated on the Up side, for better sighting by drivers.

Matlock Bath's inner (or intermediate) distant signal, situated on the Down platform just before the tunnel mouth.

In the Up (Derby) direction, the sequence of signals was:

Cromford station's distant, on the same post as Matlock Bath's starting signal on that side of Willersley tunnel (again, not shown on this diagram).

Cromford station's home signal, which because it could not be positioned in the rear of a train stopped in the station, due to the existence of Willersley tunnel, was situated at the south end of the Down platform

---

[1] In Midland Railway days the signal arms would be lowered. Signals that were raised in the 'off' position (upper quadrant) were introduced in the LMS period.

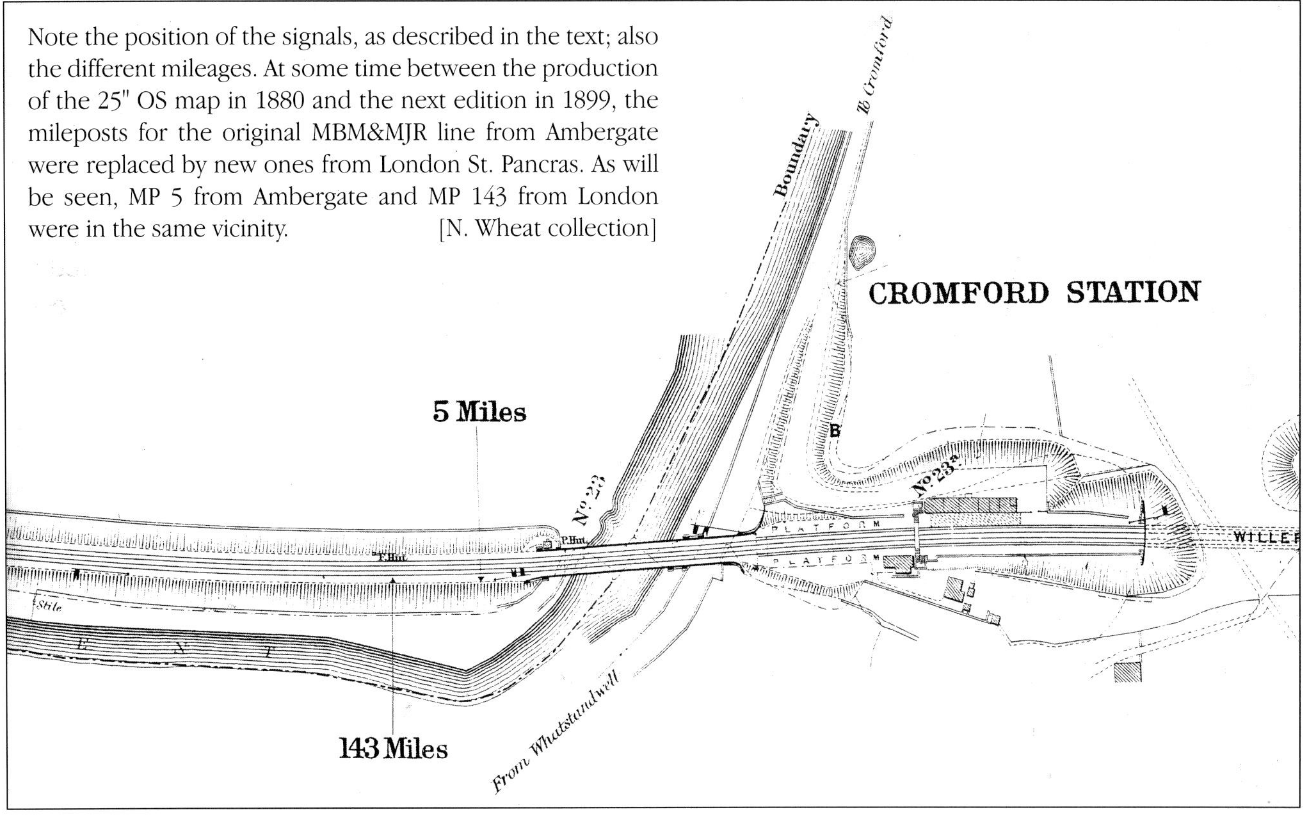

Note the position of the signals, as described in the text; also the different mileages. At some time between the production of the 25" OS map in 1880 and the next edition in 1899, the mileposts for the original MBM&MJR line from Ambergate were replaced by new ones from London St. Pancras. As will be seen, MP 5 from Ambergate and MP 143 from London were in the same vicinity. [N. Wheat collection]

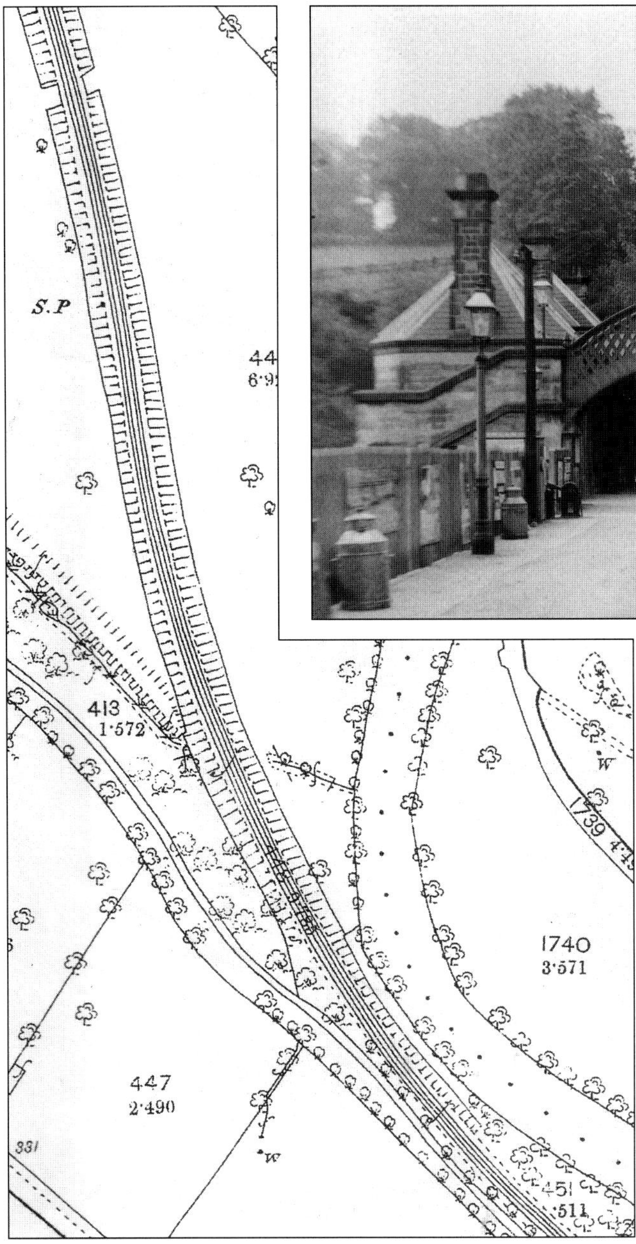

Above: Another view of Cromford station looking towards Willersley Tunnel, taken in the first decade of the 20th century. This one – besides showing the obligatory milk churns that were conveyed by rail at that time – gives a clearer view of the turnover levers on the Down side platform that controlled the station's signals. It is believed that the levers for the Up side were in the alcove to the left of the overbridge. What appears to be a wooden rail on which the levers rested in the normal position can be seen protruding from the alcove.

Left: The area around Cromford Sidings in 1880. Compare the route of the railway and the river with the 1899 version of this map on page 9. The signal post in the top left carried Cromford station's distant signal.

(again for sighting). It will be noted that a further signal is situated on that post. This was Cromford Sidings' outer distant – of which more later.

As traffic expanded, there became a need to recess trains bound for Rowsley Sidings (opened 19th March 1877) in times of congestion at that location. There was only limited accommodation at intermediate locations between Ambergate and Rowsley, while the Down slow line between Darley Dale station[2] and Church Lane Crossing did not open until 18th August 1901.

Cromford was to be the recessing location, but to provide the facilities some major engineering work was necessary. When the line was originally constructed in the late 1840s, there were some quite wide curves, which were not ideal as the speed of trains increased. The curvature of two sections of line in the Cromford area were straightened somewhat in 1884. One curve ran from the bridge over the River Derwent at the north end of Leawood Tunnel to a point just beyond the present-day sewerage works – in fact the line originally ran through part of the sewerage works area. The straightening here actually involved the demolition of the Junction Inn at what was then called Railwayend, and the replacement of a level crossing by a bridge.

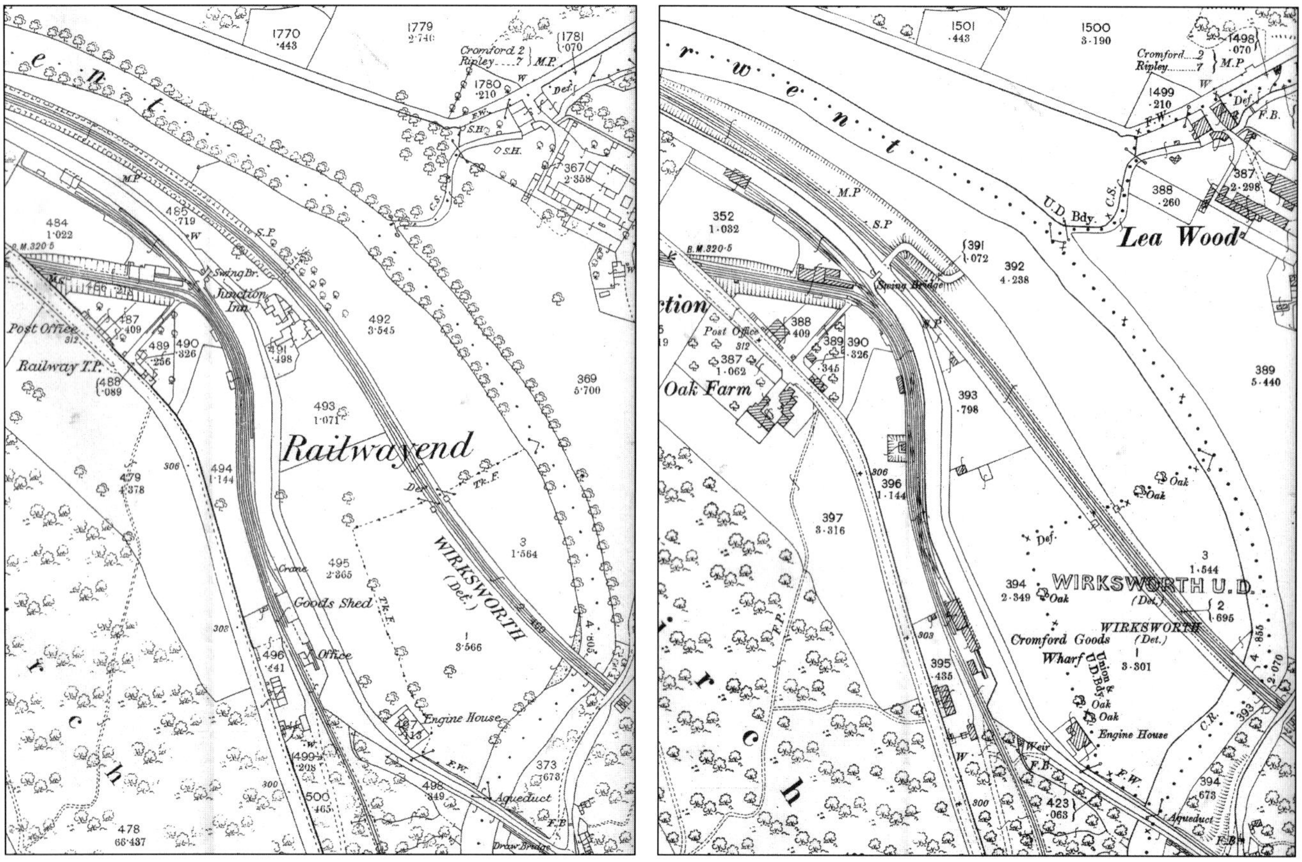

The 1880 and 1898 25" OS maps showing the original and re-aligned routes north of Leawood Tunnel. Note the slight difference in the position of the mileposts in the top left of the maps. The one in the former is 4 miles from Ambergate and in the latter 142 miles from London (see also page 37). The adjacent signal post on both maps carried High Peak Junction's Up distant; the signal post below *'Swing Bridge'* on the 1898 map carried Cromford Sidings' Down distant.

The second curve was where Cromford Sidings were eventually built. The original alignment ran along part, and in some cases to the west of the latter-day sidings. To provide the additional land required, part of the river bed was re-claimed and the river diverted in the direction of Bow Wood. The main line then took a completely new alignment. Previously, the boundary between the parishes of Cromford and Matlock followed the centre of the river. This did not change, so it can easily be determined from the OS map on page 9 where the river flowed before the Midland Railway carried out the work. The alterations to the two curves reduced the distance between High Peak Junction and Cromford station by one chain.

It would be another 6 years, however, before the signalbox and sidings were opened. The Midland Railway's weekly notice for the week ending 6th September 1890 provided the following information:

[2] Named Darley until 1st October 1890.

'Between Cromford and High Peak. On Monday next September 1st, 1890 commencing at 9am the following alterations will be made. Cromford Sidings. A new intermediate Block Telegraph Signal Post, between Cromford and High Peak Junction, will be opened and named Cromford Sidings. The signals will be:- An arm distant signal in the post of Cromford Station up home signal, an intermediate distant signal, a home signal, and a starting signal to regulate the running of trains and engines on the up main line; An arm distant signal, a home signal, and a starting signal to regulate the running of trains and engines on the down main line; A ground disc siding signal. This signal box will be closed on Sundays and Sunday nights.'

Mention has already been made of the Up distant signal being on the same post as Cromford station's Up home. It would appear from a separate notice about the signalling at Cromford station that this post previously had two home signals – presumably as an aid to sighting – and that the lower one was replaced with Cromford Siding's distant. The intermediate distant signal was 244 yards beyond this signal (see page 37), while, unusually, the home signal was a short distance beyond the signal box (see page 12). This was probably due to what was perceived as insufficient braking distance for a driver seeing the distant signal at caution when leaving Willersley Tunnel and being able to stop before the box on a falling gradient. At that time it was not feasible to pull off a signal located at the Matlock Bath end of the tunnel.

The Down distant signal was positioned at the Leawood Tunnel side of the overbridge at High Peak (see page 22). The notice about alterations at Cromford station also tells us that Cromford Siding's Down starting signal was on the same post as Cromford station's distant. From examination of OS maps, it would appear that a new post was erected at a point slightly nearer to the station than hitherto.

The new facilities at Cromford Sidings were not actually inspected until after their opening. In his report of 4th September, Major General Hutchinson RE gave the work a clean bill of health, and included the fact that the new box contained 9 working and three spare levers. It is known that it was a Type 2A box[3], a design current between 1884 and 1892. Fortunately, a copy of a Derby Signal Works ledger survives[4] which shows that a 12-lever frame for Cromford Sidings was booked out on 31st July 1890. However, an endorsement in the same handwriting reads *'from Pleasley'*. A signal box at Pleasley Colliery Sidings was replaced by two new structures on 27th July 1890, so it is possible that the frame – which was less than 5 years old – was reused at Cromford – though the box itself would probably be a new structure (see diagram on page 12).

On Monday 31st July 1891, the post bearing Cromford station's Down home and Matlock Bath's Down (outer) distant signal was replaced. It is not known how far this was from the original post. The signal post in the diagram on page 37 is that erected in 1891.

On Monday 29th January 1900 the post bearing Cromford station's Up distant signal and Matlock Bath's Down home and Up starting signals, was moved 15 yards nearer to Matlock Bath's signalbox. Almost 6 years later – on Sunday 5th November 1905 – the post bearing Cromford station's Up home signal and Cromford Sidings' Up (outer) distant was replaced. Again it is not known how far apart the two structures were. The diagram on page 37 shows the position of the later post. Cromford Sidings' Down home signal was re-sited on Monday 5th February 1906.

There then followed a major change with the abolition of all of Cromford station's signals on Sunday 27th August 1911. Cromford Sidings Up intermediate distant signal (part way down the Meadows) and Matlock Bath's Down intermediate distant signal (at the mouth of Willersley Tunnel) were also dispensed with. In addition, Matlock Bath's Down (outer) distant and Cromford Sidings' Up (outer) distant – which were on posts that also carried Cromford station's home signals, were placed on one new post at the south end of the Down platform at Cromford station. Regular passengers would have noticed quite a change when they caught their trains on the following morning.

Charles Burling, of course, came to Cromford in February 1911, so he would have witnessed these changes. Unfortunately, we cannot relate his thoughts and observations as he did not start recording matters of general railway concern until the following year.

---

[3] The classification of signal boxes by type was determined by enthusiasts in the 1980s and was not a system used by the Midland Railway.

[4] This is the only ledger known to have survived from what would have been quite a large number.

Several other developments took place in later years, although specific dates have not been traced. By the early 1930s, the two Midland Railway distant signals at the south end of Cromford station had been replaced by upper quadrant ones of LMS design. It is not known whether these were on the same post as the earlier Midland signals, or a different one. By 1950 Matlock Bath's Down distant signal had become a colour light. This meant that Cromford Sidings' Up distant signal had to be attached to a separate post, which was placed at the end of the Up platform.

Left: Class 4F No.4050 eases its way through Cromford station with a Down mixed goods in August 1934. The distant signals at the south end of the platform are now LMS upper quadrants. The locomotive carries a '20' shed code on the front, which was the number allocated to Buxton. Rowsley was a sub-shed of Buxton at this time. [E.R. Morten]
Right: Another one of E.R. Morten's excellent photographs, this time of a Down coal train hauled by Kirkby 8F No.48379 on 4th July 1953. Matlock Bath's Down distant signal is now an electric colour light, while Cromford Sidings' Up distant is a semaphore signal on that side of the line. The post can be seen straight above the engine's chimney, though the signal arm is obscured by the smoke.

One important development in LMS or early BR days was the installation of a 15-lever frame in Cromford Sidings signal box, as identified in the diagram below. It is possible that at this time a new Up outer distant was installed on the same post as Matlock Bath's Up starter (the existing distant at the south end of Cromford station becoming an inner one). It will also be noted from the diagram that the Up home signal is now positioned 33 yards before the box.

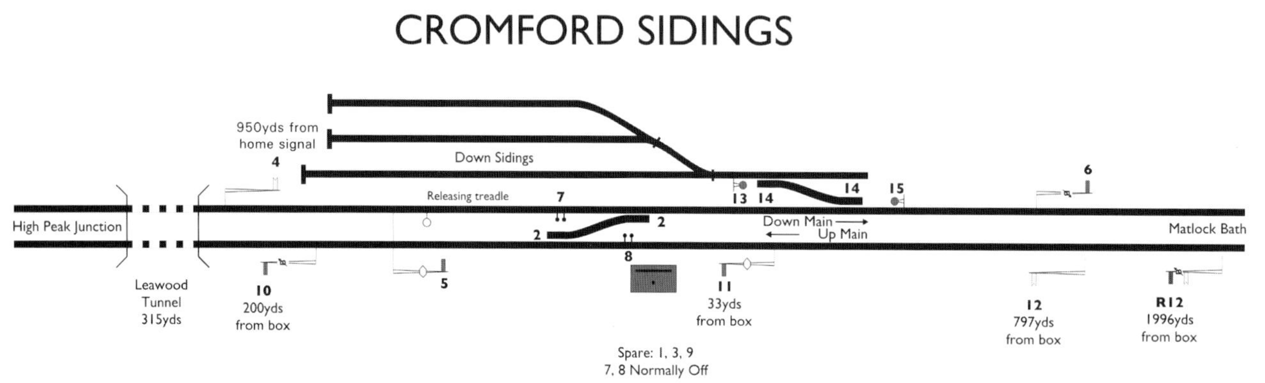

A diagram of the signalling layout at Cromford Sidings in the last few years of operation.
[drawn by Dave Harris from a sketch by Laurence Knighton.]

Standard Frame 4½" centres
Set of 15

And that more-or-less was the end of the developments. Rowsley Sidings – the main reason for the existence of Cromford Sidings signal box – closed on 27th April 1964 and quite a lot of freight traffic was diverted away from the line. The reduction in the number of trains led to both Cromford Sidings and Matlock Bath[5] signal boxes being closed from 19th December 1965, leaving the block section as High Peak Junction to Matlock. Charles Burling had come to the district in 1911 to work in Cromford Sidings box; he ended his railway career at Matlock Bath in 1947. When he died in April 1951 he could not have imagined that 15 years later both signal boxes would have closed.

[5] Goods facilities at Matlock Bath were withdrawn from 6th April 1964.

APPENDIX "B"

EXTRACTS FROM THE SETTLEMENT RELATING TO 'RATES OF WAGES, HOURS OF LABOUR AND CONDITIONS OF SERVICE' OF MIDLAND RAILWAY SIGNALMEN INTRODUCED ON 1ST JULY 1912

Signalmen, &c.

1. *Hours of Duty.*

All booked turns of duty exceeding 10 working hours per day will be abolished, and the standard hours of Signalmen, Assistant Signalmen, and Train Recorders, will be 8, 9, or 10 per day, without booked intervals for meals, according to the box at which they are employed.

The standard daily hours of Porter Signalmen will be 11 per day, less 1½ hours for meals, which will be arranged at reasonable times convenient to the Company's business.

As far as practicable the standard hours will be adhered to, but when necessary, men will be required to remain on duty for longer periods. Time worked beyond the standard hours on any day will be paid for as overtime at the rate stipulated in Clause 5.

2. *Rates of Wages.*

Signalmen, Assistant Signalmen, and Train Recorders.

The system of paying an annual bonus to Signalmen in recognition of satisfactory conduct will be discontinued, and the amount of the bonus will be included in the weekly rates of wages fixed for the respective classes.

The existing designations of the several classes of signal cabins will be abandoned, and all cabins will be placed in either Class No. 1, 2, 3, 4, 5, 6, 7, 8, 9, 10, or 11.

The standard rates of pay for six days' duty will be as shown in the annexed schedule subject to the conditions herein mentioned.

Upon these revised scales coming into force, Signalmen will be advanced to the wages given for the class shown as corresponding to that in which they are now included.

Porter Signalmen.

The rate of pay of Porter Signalmen will be 21*s*. 6*d*. per week ; with the exception of men employed at the undermentioned stations, at which the rate will be 20*s*. 6*d*. :—

Ingleton ; Addingham ; Embsay (Station Cabin) ; Wirksworth ; Idridgehay ; Chellaston ; Weston-on-Trent ; Castle Donington ; Worthington ; Streetly ; Walsall Wood ; Brownhills ; Beckford ; Malvern Wells ; Upton-on-Severn ; Ryeford ; Yate (Single Line Junction) ; Farnsfield ; Broughton Astley ; Raunds ; Piddington ; Turvey ; Southill ; Shefford ; Hitchin.

Payment of wages will be made weekly, and will be calculated upon the number of days actually worked, with the exception of those weeks in which men take their annual holidays.

Men required to live in the London District (St. Pancras to Hendon) will receive an allowance of 3*s*. per week over the wages noted herein for the London stations and depôts. This allowance will be paid continuously to all men regularly employed and living in the London area, except to men absent from duty without permission, or for disciplinary reasons.

3. *Each turn of duty to stand by itself.*

For the purpose of calculating the week's wages, including overtime earnings, each turn of duty will stand by itself.

4. *Payment for signing on duty.*

Men who sign on by order for a scheduled day's duty, and are actually employed for any part of the day, will be paid not less than a full day's wages.

5. *Overtime.*

Time made in addition to the standard day's work will be paid for at the rate of ordinary time and a quarter, calculated on the basis of the standard working hours for the day.

6. *Sunday duty, Christmas Day, and Good Friday.*

All time worked between midnight and midnight on Sundays, Christmas Day, and Good Friday, whether forming part of, or in addition to, the scheduled week's work, will be calculated on the standard working hours, and will be paid at ordinary rate and a quarter. Men called on duty for a turn on either of the days named, and working less than the stipulated hours for a standard day, will be paid for the actual time worked at rate and a quarter, but in no case will a man employed on either of those days receive less than a full day's wage calculated at his week-day rate.

When men are required to book on duty three or more times on either Sunday, Christmas Day, or Good Friday, in order to perform the scheduled workings for those days, they will receive not less than a full day's wages calculated at rate and a quarter, even though the number of hours actually worked is less than the standard day.

7. *Intervals between turns of duty.*

So far as the necessities of the service permit, arrangements will be made for men who have completed a turn of duty to be allowed not less than nine hours for rest before being required to again sign on for work.

In the event of any man being called out for duty before the expiration of the nine hours' rest, he will be paid for the unexpired portion of the nine hours at the rate of time and a half. This regulation will not apply in the following cases :—

(*a*) To men, who in making the weekly change in their turns of duty, have a less interval than nine hours.

(*b*) To cases of emergency when, owing to breakdown, fog, &c., men are called out specially within four hours after completing the scheduled day's work. In such cases, men will be treated as having continued on duty, and will be paid at rate and a quarter for the time between the close of the scheduled day's work and the completion of the special duty, and in no such case will a man receive less than half a day's pay at rate and a quarter.

8. *Holidays.*

(*a*) Annual.

Holidays without loss of pay will be allowed each year at such times as may be convenient to the Company, on the following scale :—

Three days after one year's service. Five days after 10 years' service.
Four „ „ five years' „ Six „ „ 15 „ „

This privilege is withdrawable at any time at the discretion of the Company.

(*b*) Bank, Public or Local.

Those men for whom the Company has no work on Bank, Public, or Local holidays, or at other times, will not be paid wages for those days.

9. *Men performing superior duties.*

When men are required by the Company to temporarily take over the duties and responsibilities of a superior grade for a quarter of a day or more, they will be paid, whilst so employed, at the minimum rate of the scale applicable to the superior grade, and in no case at a rate less than 1*s.* above their ordinary weekly wage.

Men who, from time to time, are called upon to temporarily perform the duties of a superior post will, after being so employed for 313 days, be entitled to count each further complete 313 days' work in the superior position as one year for the purpose of qualifying for advancement in wages in accordance with the increments of the scale applicable to that post.

When necessary to place men temporarily to superior duties, the Company's Officers will select those they consider the most suitable for the position, and, in so doing, will, as far as consistent, pay regard to seniority.

This clause does not apply to men temporarily acting for short periods during the absence for meals, &c., of men in superior grades, nor to cases in which men perform necessary and regular Sunday duty in turns.

10. *Men performing other duties.*

If, from any cause, the Company are unable to find regular work for a man in his own grade, they will, as far as possible, offer him employment, if available, in any inferior grade for which, in their opinion, he is suited, and whilst so employed he will be subject to the conditions as to hours, wages, &c., applicable to the position occupied.

The earnings of men employed temporarily, for the convenience of the Company, in an inferior position, will be calculated on the basis of the conditions applicable to their own grade, but they will actually work, for the time being, under the regulations as to hours, &c., of the men they relieve.

11. *Uniform.*

The Company will supply each man with a complete suit of uniform and an extra pair of trousers annually, and with an overcoat every two years, as at present. The quality of the material, and the style of the clothing, will be such as the Company consider most suitable.

Schedule of Wages of Signalmen, Assistant Signalmen, and Adult Train Recorders.

Signalmen.

Class of Cabin.		Proposed Rates.
Present.	Proposed.	Fixed Rate.
		s. d.
3rd C. ... ... 3rd B. ... ... 3rd A.	1st.	24 6
New Class	2nd.	25 6
Second	3rd.	26 6
New Class	4th.	27 6
1st C.	5th.	28 0
1st B.	6th.	29 0
1st A.	7th.	30 0
Special C.	8th.	31 0
„ B.	9th.	32 0
„ A.	10th.	33 0
Extra Special	11th.	34 0

Note that in addition to the 11 grades, specific rates of pay from 35/- to 37/- per week were granted to signalmen employed at 14 '*exceptionally rated cabins*'. Assistant signalmen at 28 boxes were also specially allocated to one of the new 11 grades.

APPENDIX "C"

SUMMARY OF SETTLEMENT RELATING TO MIDLAND RAILWAY SIGNALLING GRADES 13TH FEBRUARY 1914

In section 2 there are three entries at the beginning of February 1914 relating to meetings about a *'signalmen's movement'*, one of which mentions the *'Company's offer'*. Discussions on improvements in signalmen's conditions of service had obviously been taking place for some time. There had been a meeting of the Conciliation Board No.2 at Derby on 28th January, which led to the local meetings on 3rd and 4th February. The one Charles mentioned on the 10th of the month actually concluded the agreement, with new arrangements being introduced on Friday 13th February[1].

It is surprising that Charles did not record the terms of the settlement, but by mentioning the meetings he would have been fully aware of what was happening. The report on the introduction of the settlement in the *Railway Review* refers to an application from signalmen (see page 32), and therefore he may not have seen the finer detail as particularly newsworthy – or perhaps he just forgot to make an entry.

The main changes were increases in the number of grades from 11 to 13, and the weekly wage of most signalmen. A summary was provided, as follows:

Existing Grade	**Revised Grade**	**Revised Rate of Pay**
No.1 (formerly 3rd C)	No.1 – comprising cabins on appended list	24s.6d
No.1 (formerly 3rd B)	No.2 – comprising former 3rd B and all cabins in former 3rd C not included in new Class 1	25s.0d
No.1 (formerly 3rd A)	No.3	25s.6d
No.2	No.4	26s.6d
No.3	No.5	27s.6d
No.4	No.6	28s.6d
No.5	No.7	29s.0d
No.6	No.8	30s.0d
No.7	No.9	31s.0d
No.8	No.10	32s.0d
No.9	No.11	33s.0d
No.10	No.12	34s.0d
No.11	No.13	35s.0d

The list relating to the new No.1 Grade concerned *'nearly 40 men'*. These men received no advance in their wages. Those in the new No.2 Grade received 6d more per week, while all other grades received 1s.0d per week. Cromford Sidings was previously in the No.4 Grade, so this would have now changed to No.6 Grade.

In addition, there was a list of 14 exceptionally rated cabins – the occupants of which also received an increase of 1s.0d per week – and a list of boxes where assistant signalmen were employed, with the grades to which they were allocated. Porter signalmen were also included in the agreement.

Amongst other clauses was one about the minimum day. This stated that anyone who signed on duty would not receive less than an ordinary day's pay, and that no-one would be called to sign on duty on more than one occasion for a day's wages, other than *'fifth men'* working between two 10 hour boxes. They would continue to work two periods of 4 hours each, separated by an interval of not more that 4 hours, as at present. This gives an insight into the working at Cromford Sidings, which was a 10 hour box (see Section 1 – 19.12.1911).

[1] At first sight, this appears to be an unusual day to start an agreement, but at that time Midland Railway employees were paid on a Thursday, so this would be the start of a new week for payment purposes.

APPENDIX "D"
ALTERATIONS TO SIGNAL BOX CLASSIFICATION AND SIGNALMEN'S PAY 1920 TO 1922

Whilst an agreement of 1st February 1919 conceded the principle of the 8-hour day and the standard 48-hour working week, this did not resolve all of the railwaymen's grievances that had been 'put on hold' during the war. Following a national strike from 29th September to 6th October of the same year, there then followed a series of meetings and agreements relating to different grades of staff, some of which were not properly concluded until 1922.

The initial agreement relating to signalmen was made on 20th March 1920, backdated to 1st January. This reduced the number of signalling grades from 13 to 6 – subsequently increased to 7, with the addition of a 'Special' grade. However, there was no formula to link former grades with the new ones. Instead, the grading of every box was to be determined by a marks assessment.

Pre-set marks were given for every possible activity in a signal box – e.g. 1 mark for pulling or replacing a lever; 6 marks for bell signals associated with a through train; 3 marks for entries in the train register book. A survey was carried out at each box on a selected weekday and the total number of marks calculated.

To eliminate the effects of peaks and troughs by using such a limited sample, the numbers of trains dealt with on 6 weekdays in each of four specified months preceding the taking of the marks was determined. The daily figures were added and then divided by 24 to give an average number of trains per day. This figure was compared with the number of trains run on the day the marks were taken and the total marks re-calculated on a pro-rata basis.

Marks for telephone and telegraph messages, and for signal lamp cleaning and trimming were analysed separately, where applicable, and added to the marks calculated for train running. The grand total was then divided by the number of hours the box was open each day, to arrive at an average marks per hour figure. This was then used to determine the grading of the box – and the signalmen who worked in it.

The large number of signal boxes on the British rail system, made it inevitable that the process would take quite some time to complete, while it was also accepted that minor adjustments would be made from experience gained in the exercise. In the meantime signalmen were to be paid their pre-war rates, plus 33s.0d per week war bonus (for inflation), and an additional 5s.0d per week granted as part of the agreement, backdated to 1st January. In Charles Burling's case, this would mean a weekly rate of 66s.6d. This rate was to remain in operation until 30th September 1920. New inclusive rates of pay were to be introduced from 1st October based on the inflation rate of 125% as at 1st January 1920[1]. However, if the level of inflation was more or less than 125%, then a payment or deduction of 1s.0d would be made for each 5-point variation, based on the September figures.

At this time, the level of inflation was around 160%, so the men would have received a further increment.

Inflation peaked at 169% at the beginning of January 1921. Thereafter it fell gradually – and so did the men's wages. In May 1922, when the final agreement was made, the level of inflation had fallen to around 85% of pre-war levels and the rates of pay had also reduced.

A table produced on 1st May 1922 gave details of the relationship between the average numbers of marks and the then standard rates of pay:

Class	Average No. of marks per hour	Standard Rate per week (A)	(B)
Special	375 and over	75s.0d	72s.6d
First	300 – 374	70s.0d	67s.0d
Second	225 – 299	65s.0d	62s.6d
Third	150 – 224	60s.0d	57s.6d
Fourth	75 – 149	55s.0d	52s.6d
Fifth	30 – 74	50s.0d	48s.0d
Sixth	1 – 29	48s.0d	48s.0d

Scale (A) applied to boxes that normally controlled passenger trains.
Scale (B) applied to boxes that did not normally deal with such trains.

[1] These appeared to be fairly close to the rates paid to the men when the agreement was signed. Cromford Sidings would be graded Class 4, the October 1920 rate for which was 65s.0d.

Relief signalmen were paid as follows: Special – 80s.0d Class 1 – 70s.0d Class 2 – 60s.0d

By now the standard (or railway) rate had incorporated much of the inflation caused by the war and its aftermath. Cromford Sidings signal box became Class 4 in the new classifications, at a weekly rate of 55s.0d – almost twice the pre-war wage. Charles Burling became a relief signalman on 17th April 1923. This was a Class 2 post, so he would have received a rise of 5s.0d per week on taking up those duties.

APPENDIX "E"

A WILLERSLEY TUNNEL INCIDENT – THE DEATH OF WILLIAM BODEN ON MONDAY 18TH NOVEMBER 1912

At about 3.40pm on Monday 18th November 1912, men working in Matlock Bath Goods Yard saw 48 year old Second Ganger William Boden walking along the Down (Matlock direction) line from the north end of Willersley Tunnel in a state of physical distress. He started rambling and wanted to know where he was and how he got there.

The men sent for Station Master Henry Lovatt, who at first believed that Boden had had an attack of apoplexy. An ambulance was called and he was taken to Whitworth Hospital (situated between Matlock and Darley Dale). He was seen at 7.15pm that evening by Dr Moxon, who found that he was suffering form severe shock and had no recollection of any incident. He had a fracture of the upper left arm and 9th rib[1] on his left side, and a slight injury to his lung. Unfortunately, his condition worsened and he died at 9.20am on the following morning. The cause of death was given as *'concussion followed by shock, which was accelerated by exposure'*.

At the coroner's inquest held at 2.30pm on Wednesday 20th November, William Dale[2], the Inspector of Permanent Way at Matlock Bath, said that Boden would examine the road through the tunnel twice a day. He had been employed by the Midland Railway for 25 years and had covered the Cromford length for 17 or 18 years, but had been conversant with Willersley Tunnel for all his working life.

Thomas Cooper, the Station Master at Cromford said that he last saw Boden at the Cromford end of the tunnel around 2.30pm. At 3.27pm a light engine passed through the tunnel and it was believed that he was struck by this engine and thrown a considerable distance, sustaining the injuries described above. The shock would have affected his memory. In his partially concussed state he had either crawled or walked to the open air at Matlock Bath station.

A verdict of *'accidental death'* was returned by the jury.

Left: The Cromford end of Willersley Tunnel in LMS days, with Compound No.1060 arriving on a Derby bound passenger train. The type of shed plate on the engine's smokebox indicates that it is pre-1935. This is where William Boden would have entered the tunnel.

Right: The line at the north end of Willersley Tunnel runs through a small cutting, then curves right to pass through Matlock Bath station. This shot taken on 24th May 1952 shows Class 5XP Jubilee No.45628 *Somaliland* at the head of a Manchester-bound express. The train has just negotiated the curve leading from the tunnel. The Goods Yard, where William Boden staggered to, is on the right. [E.R. Morten]

[1] Subsequently diagnosed has having three broken ribs.

[2] Left Matlock Bath for a job at Ashchurch in December 1914 (see main text, Section 2).

Appendix "F"
TRAINS PASSING CROMFORD SIDINGS SIGNAL BOX JULY, AUGUST AND SEPTEMBER 1914

[Times are estimated based on passing / arrival / departure times at adjacent locations – other than when timed to be recessed on the Down line]

Abbreviations

Days: EWD = Each weekday; O after other days = Only; X = excepted; Q = runs when required.
Type of train: EBV = Engine & Brakevan; ECS = Empty Coaching Stock; EF = Express Freight; Eties = Empties; Exp = Express; Min = Mineral train; Pass = (slow) Passenger train; Per = Perishable; SF = Stopping Freight; TF = Through Freight.

DOWN LINE

Time	Days	Type of train	From	To	Arrive	Depart / pass	Notes
Weekdays							
5.35pm	FSX	EF	Somers Town	Rowsley		12.23am	At Cromford MSX
11.27pm	FO	EF	Lenton Jn.	Rowsley		12.23am	At Cromford SO
10.05pm	FSX	EF	Duddeston Sidings	Huskisson		12.29am	At Cromford MSX
10.05pm	FO	EF	Duddeston Sidings	Rowsley		12.29am	At Cromford SO
12.00mn	MX	Min	Derby St. Marys	Rowsley		12.45am	
1.00am	MX	Exp	Derby	Manchester Central		1.23am	
1.45am	MX	Min	Ambergate	Rowsley		2.02am	
10.40pm	SX	EF	Birmingham Cen.	Ancoats		2.37am	At Cromford MX
1.25am	MX	EF	Leicester	Rowsley		2.48am	
1.55am	MX	Min	Kirkby	Rowsley		3.15am	
2.56am	EWD Q	Exp	Trent	Manchester Cen / Vic		3.36am	Standard excursion Runs as reqd.
2.08am	EWD	Min	Beeston	Rowsley		3.40am	See Note 1
12.15am	EWD	Exp	London St. Pancras	Manchester Central		3.57am	
3.35am	MX	Exp	Derby	Stockport TD		4.06am	
2.30am	MX	Min	Tibshelf Junction	Buxton		4.17am	See SO and standard excursion entries below.
11.45pm	FO	Exp	Bristol TM	Manchester Cen / Vic		4.32am	Standard excursion. At Cromford SO 4th July to 19th September.
2.30am	SO	Min	Tibshelf Junction	Buxton	4.20am	4.35am	Timings on days when 11.45pm FO standard excursion from Bristol runs.
3.20am	MX	Min	Kirkby	Ashton Road		4.48am	
3.20am	MX	Min	Toton	Rowsley		4.58am	
1.45am	MSX	TF	Burton	Heaton Mersey		5.12am	
3.25am	MO	Exp	Leicester	Blackpool T. Rd.		5.19am	See Note 2
2.40am	MX	Exp	London St. Pancras	Manchester Central		5.37am	
5.33am	MX	Min	Ambergate	Rowsley		5.50am	
5.10am	MX	Min	Derby St. Marys	Rowsley		5.59am	
4.50am	MX	Min	Kirkby	Northwich		6.07am	Suspended
5.06am	MSX Q	TF	Wetmore Sidings	Cheadle Sidings		6.27am	
5.10am	MO	Min	Toton	Rowsley		6.43am	Suspended
5.50am	EWD Q	TF	Chaddesden	Rowsley		6.45am	
11.35pm	SX	TF	St. Pancras Goods	Rowsley		6.57am	EF to Derby St. Marys
4.30am	MX	Min	Avenue Sidings	Rowsley		7.07am	
4.40am	MO	Exp	Leicester	Liverpool Central		7.11am	See Note 3
6.55am	EWD	Exp	Derby	Chinley		7.19am	
6.05am	MO	Min	Staveley	Rowsley		7.36am	
6.55am	MO	Min	Derby St. Marys	Rowsley		7.45am	
7.07am	MX	Min	Little Eaton Jn.	Rowsley		7.45am	
7.10am	EWD	Pass	Derby	Manchester Central		7.51am	
7.17am	TFO	Per	Derby	Bakewell		7.59am	Runs to 25th August.
4.50am	EWD	Exp	London St. Pancras	Manchester Central		8.29am	
8.12am	SO	Exp	Derby	Blackpool		8.35am	Runs 8th August to 26th September.
6.40am	EWD	Min	Toton	Rowsley		9.15am	
8.35am	EWD	Exp	Leicester	Manchester Central		9.58am	

1 Recessed at Ambergate and runs forward 7 mins later when 2.56am standard excursion from Trent runs.

2 Standard excursion. Runs 6th July to 28th September (except 3rd August). Also conveys portion from Nottingham, depart 4.05am.

3 Standard excursion. Runs 13th July to 7th September (except 3rd August). Also conveys portion from Nottingham, depart 6.00am.

Time	Days	Type of train	From	To	Arrive	Depart / pass	Notes
7.38am	MSO	Exp	Camp Hill	Rowsley		10.07am	See Note 4
1.35am	MO	Eties	Brent	Rowsley		10.11am	
9.45am	EWD	Pass	Derby	Manchester Central		10.21am	
10.30am	EWD	Pass	Derby	Buxton		10.51am	
9.15am	EWD	SF	Derby St. Marys	Rowsley	10.45am	10.57am	
9.00am	MO	Min	Kirkby	Northwich		11.15am	
8.45am	MSX	Min	Kirkby	Rowsley		11.15am	
10.36am	SO	Exp	Nottingham	Blackpool		11.21am	
10.47am	EWD	Exp	Nottingham	Manchester Central		11.33am	
8.45am	SO	Min	Kirkby	Rowsley	11.15am	11.36am	
10.30am	WThX	Exp	Leicester	Blackpool		11.51am	
10.25am	MX	Min	Kirkby	Rowsley	11.45am	11.54am	
8.55am	EWD	Min	Staveley	Rowsley		12.02pm	
11.20am	EWD	Min	Tibshelf Junction	Rowsley		12.23pm	
10.00am	SX	Exp	London St. Pancras	Manchester Central		12.42pm	
12.05pm	EWD	Pass	Derby	Buxton		1.04pm	Held at Ambergate for connections.
10.06am	EWD	Exp	London St. Pancras	Manchester Central		1.22pm	
1.10pm	SX	Exp	Derby	Liverpool Central		1.32pm	
10.33am	SO	Exp	London St. Pancras	Liverpool Central		1.32pm	
1.16pm	SO	Exp	Derby	Liverpool Central		1.38pm	
12.15pm	SX	Min	Kirkby	Ashton Road		1.46pm	
12.15pm	SO	Min	Kirkby	Ashton Road		1.51pm	
12.40pm	SX	Min	Derby St. Marys	Rowsley		1.52pm	
1.21pm	SX	Pass	Derby	Rowsley		2.00pm	
1.21pm	SO	Pass	Derby	Buxton		2.00pm	
1.10pm	SO	Pass	Burton	Rowsley		2.06pm	Standard excursion. Runs 4th July to 5th Sept. (except 1st and 8th Aug.).
2.02pm	SX	Min	Ambergate	Rowsley		2.17pm	
1.25pm	ThO	Pass	Nottingham	Rowsley		2.20pm	Standard excursion. Runs 2nd July to 10th September.
1.26pm	ThO	Exp	Sheffield	Rowsley		2.30pm	Standard excursion. Runs 2nd July to 10th September.
2.15pm	SO	Min	Ambergate	Rowsley		2.30pm	
12.50pm	TO	TF	Chaddesden	Hassop		2.32pm	
11.35am	WO	Exp	London St. Pancras	Rowsley		2.33pm	Standard excursion. Runs 1st July to 9th September.
12.00nn	EWD	Exp	London St. Pancras	Manchester Central		2.57pm	
12.07pm	EWD	Exp	London St. Pancras	Manchester Victoria		3.07pm	
12.12pm	EWD	Exp	Nottingham	Buxton		3.30pm	
12.05pm	MX	Min	Beeston	Rowsley	3.25pm	3.35pm	
12.15pm	EWD	Exp	London St. Pancras	Manchester Central		3.57pm	
12.18pm	SO Q	Exp	London St. Pancras	Manchester Central		4.04pm	
2.35pm	EWD	Min	Kirkby	Rowsley		4.11pm	Runs 35 mins later on Saturdays when required.
3.43pm	EWD	Pass	Derby	Manchester Central		4.25pm	
11.38am	FO	Exp	Bristol TM	Manchester Cen / Vic		4.28pm	See Note 5
4.15pm	EWD	Min	Ambergate	Rowsley		4.35pm	See also entry below.
4.20pm	FO	Min	Ambergate	Rowsley		4.40pm	Timings on days when 11.38am FO standard excursion from Bristol runs.
4.25pm	EWD	Pass	Derby	Matlock		4.55pm	
4.45pm	TFX	ECS	Derby	Cromford Sidings	5.08pm		See Note 6
2.30pm	EWD	Exp	London St. Pancras	Manchester Central		5.16pm	
5.02pm	EWD	Exp	Derby	Manchester Victoria		5.22pm	
2.33pm	WFSO	Exp	London St. Pancras	Manchester Cen / Vic; Liverpool Cen; Blackburn (SO)		5.35pm	See Note 7
4.20pm	EWD	Min	Tibshelf Junction	Rowsley		5.43pm	See Note 8
5.38pm	EWD	Exp	Derby	Manchester Central		5.56pm	
6.15pm	TFX	ECS	Cromford Sidings	Cromford Station		6.15pm	See Note 9

4 Standard excursion. Runs Mondays 6th July to 24th August (except 3rd August), Saturdays 4th & 11th July and 29th August, and as required. Also conveys portion from Wolverhampton, depart 7.30am, on specified days.

5 Standard excursion. Runs 10th July to 18th September. Also conveys portion from Bath, depart 11.25am.

6 To work 6.18pm Pass Cromford to Manchester Victoria. Runs until 31st August.

7 Standard excursion. Runs Wednesday 5th August; two Fridays in July, August and September; all Saturdays except 1st & 8th August.

8 Recessed at Ambergate and runs forward 3 mins later when 2.33pm standard excursion from St. Pancras runs.

9 To work 6.18pm Pass Cromford to Manchester Victoria (Exp from Rowsley). Runs until 31st August.

Time	Days	Type of train	From	To	Arrive	Depart / pass	Notes
5.45pm	EWD	Pass	Derby	Rowsley		6.29pm	
6.38pm	EWD	Min	Ambergate	Rowsley		6.51pm	
6.30pm	SO	ECS	Derby	Cromford Sidings	6.58pm		To work 7.40pm Express Matlock Bath to Manchester Central.
4.30pm	EWD	Exp	London St. Pancras	Manchester Central		7.31pm	
7.35pm	SO	ECS	Cromford Sidings	Matlock Bath		7.35pm	See Note 10
6.35pm	EWD	Min	Derby St. Marys	Rowsley	7.21pm	7.35pm	See also SO entry below.
7.20pm	EWD	Exp	Derby	Manchester Central		7.44pm	
6.35pm	SO	Min	Derby St. Marys	Rowsley	7.21pm	7.50pm	Until 29th August. Thereafter as EWD entry above.
7.43pm	SO	Eties	Ambergate	Matlock		7.59pm	
5.35pm	SX	Exp	London St. Pancras	Manchester Central		8.24pm	
8.15pm	EWD	Pass	Derby	Manchester Central		8.41pm	
6.10pm	FO	Exp	London St. Pancras	Liverpool Central		8.49pm	
7.35pm	EWD	Exp	Leicester	Manchester Central		8.52pm	
6.40pm	SO	Min	Derby	Rowsley	8.12pm	8.53pm	
7.15pm	EWD	Min	Seymour Junction	Rowsley		9.06pm	Leaves Seymour Junction at 7.20pm on Saturdays.
8.40pm	SX	Min	Derby St. Marys	Rowsley		9.17pm	
6.30pm	EWD	Exp	London St. Pancras	Manchester Central		9.26pm	
8.10pm	SX	Min	Kirkby	Hartford		9.44pm	
9.35pm	EWD	Min	Ambergate	Rowsley		10.00pm	Calls High Peak Junction.
9.50pm	SX	Min	Ambergate	Matlock		10.06pm	
9.00pm	SX	Min	Kirkby	Rowsley		10.16pm	Suspended
8.45pm	SO	Min	Tibshelf Junction	Buxton		10.16pm	
9.08pm	EWD	TF	Wetmore Sidings	Huskisson		10.25pm	
9.45pm	SX	EF	Nottingham	Brunswick		10.51pm	
10.10pm	FSX	EF	Nottingham	Huskisson		11.13pm	
9.25pm	SX	EF	Duddeston Sidings	Rowsley		11.23pm	
11.00pm	SO	Pass	Derby	Rowsley		11.27pm	
8.55pm	SX	TF	Leicester	Ancoats		11.48pm	EF from Leicester to Derby St. Marys and from Rowsley to Ancoats.
Sundays							
8.00pm	SO	Min	Leicester	Ancoats		12.22am	
1.25am	Sun	Exp	Derby	Manchester Central		1.48am	
10.15pm	SO	TF	Lawley Street	Rowsley		2.10am	
2.15am	Sun	Min	Derby St. Marys	Rowsley		2.51am	
1.05am	Sun	TF	Nottingham	Brunswick		3.08am	
11.40pm	SO	TF	Leicester	Rowsley		3.18am	
1.45am	Sun	TF	Burton	Heaton Mersey		4.24am	
12.15am	Sun	Exp	London St. Pancras	Manchester Central		3.57am	
3.45am	Sun	Exp	Derby	Liverpool Central		4.09am	
10.35pm	SO	EF	St. Pancras Goods	Ancoats		4.41am	
10.35pm	SO	TF	Somers Town	Rowsley		5.34am	
4.15am	Sun	TF	Saltley	Rowsley		7.16am	
7.10am	Sun	Pass	Derby	Manchester Central		7.44am	
12.30am	Sun	TF	Somers Town	Rowsley		9.29am	
10.20am	Sun	Pass	Derby	Rowsley		10.51am	
2.05pm	Sun	Pass	Derby	Buxton		2.36pm	
12.00nn	Sun	Exp	London St. Pancras	Manchester Central		3.15pm	
12.15pm	Sun	Exp	London St. Pancras	Liverpool Central		3.46pm	
5.55pm	Sun	ECS	Derby	Matlock Bath		6.24pm	To work 6.33pm Exp Matlock Bath to Manchester Central.
6.20pm	Sun	Exp	Derby	Manchester Central		6.41pm	Also conveys portion for Liverpool.
6.55pm	Sun	Pass	Derby	Manchester Central		7.29pm	
6.30pm	Sun	Exp	London St. Pancras	Manchester Central		9.34pm	
7.30pm	Sun	TF	Lawley Street	Ancoats		10.45pm	
4.0pm	Sun	TF	Somers Town	Rowsley		11.38pm	

[10] To work 7.40pm Exp Matlock Bath to Manchester Central. Runs until 29th August.

[11] Standard excursion – runs as required. Also conveys portion from Manchester Vic., depart 12.20am

[12] Locally known as *'The Joe Wright'* after the guard who worked the train from 1886 to 1928.

[13] Standard excursion. Runs 3rd July to 18th September. Also conveys portion from Manchester Vic., depart 10.10am. Freight services regulated slightly.

UP LINE

Time	Days	Type of train	From	To	Pass	Notes
Weekdays						
11.55pm	SX	Eties	Rowsley	Ambergate	12.15am	At Cromford MX
12.25am	MX	EF	Rowsley	Lawley Street	12.38am	
12.40am	SO	TF	Rowsley	Lawley Street	12.55am	
12.40am	MX	Eties	Rowsley	Kirkby	1.02am	Suspended
7.17pm	FSX	EF	Huskisson	Saltley	1.15am	At Cromford MSX
12.01am	MX	Exp	Manchester Central	London St. Pancras	1.25am	
11.32pm	SX	Exp	Liverpool Central	Derby	1.33am	At Cromford MX
1.33am	MX	EF	Rowsley	St. Pancras Goods	1.45am	
9.35pm	SX	EF	Philips Park	Birmingham Central	1.53am	At Cromford MX
8.15pm	MX	EF	Ancoats	Leicester	2.02am	At Cromford MX
12.25am	EWD Q	Exp	Manchester Central	Trent	2.10am	See Note 11
6.30pm	FSX	EF	Alexandra	Nottingham	2.37am	At Cromford MSX
2.25am	SO	EF	Rowsley	Nottingham	2.37am	
2.45am	MX	TF	Rowsley	Derby St. Marys	3.00am	
3.22am	MX	Eties	Rowsley	Ambergate	3.42am	
3.50am	MX	TF	Rowsley	Wellingborough	4.05am	
4.00am	MX	TF	Rowsley	Lawley Street	4.15am	
4.30am	MO	TF	Rowsley	Chaddesden	4.45am	
9.03pm	SX	TF	Huskisson	Burton	4.45am	At Cromford MX
9.35pm	SX	TF	Brunswick	Nottingham	5.00am	At Cromford MX
5.00am	MX	TF	Rowsley	Mansfield	5.15am	
2.40am	MX	TF	Cheadle Sidings	Burton	5.27am	
6.00am	MX	TF	Rowsley	Leicester	6.15am	
1.55am	MX	Eties	Hartford	Kirkby	7.07am	
3.30am	MO	Eties	Ashton Road	Kirkby	7.32am	
7.15am	MX	Eties	Rowsley	Beeston	7.32am	
7.33am	EWD	Pass	Bakewell	Derby	7.58am	See Note 12
1.30am	MSX	Eties	Ashton Road	Kirkby	8.08am	
3.15am	MX	Eties	Northwich	Kirkby	8.17am	Suspended
7.30am	EWD	Exp	Manchester Central	London St. Pancras	8.34am	
8.30am	TO	Eties	Rowsley	Chaddesden	8.42am	
8.19am	EWD	Pass	Millers Dale	Derby	8.58am	
9.05am	TFO	ECS	Bakewell	Derby	9.25am	
8.55am	MX	Min	Rowsley	Chaddesden	9.32am	Calls at Matlock.
8.37am	EWD	Exp	Chinley	Derby	9.47am	
9.40am	MO	Eties	Rowsley	Toton	9.57am	Suspended
9.20am	EWD	Exp	Manchester Central	London St. Pancras	10.29am	
8.37am	TFX	Pass	Manchester Victoria	Derby	10.42am	Runs until 31st August.
10.06am	EWD	Pass	Buxton	Derby	10.56am	
11.05am	EWD	ECS	Matlock Bath	Derby	11.09am	After working 8.55am Manchester Central to Matlock Bath.
10.10am	SX	Exp	Manchester Central	London St. Pancras	11.17am	
10.15am	EWD	Exp	Manchester Central	London St. Pancras	11.34am	
10.55am	MX	Eties	Rowsley	Avenue	11.42am	See 10.25am standard excursion from Manchester.
10.25am	FO	Exp	Manchester Central	Derby	11.46am	See Note 13
6.30am	MTX	Eties	Cheadle Sidings	Blackwell Sidings	11.50am	See 10.25am standard excursion from Manchester.
11.35am	EWD	Eties	Rowsley	Toton	11.55am	See 10.25am standard excursion from Manchester.
10.56am	EWD	Exp	Manchester Central	Derby	12.12pm	
11.25am	EWD	Pass	Buxton	Derby	12.31am	
12.20pm	EWD	SF	Rowsley	Chaddesden	12.43pm	
12.00nn	EWD	Exp	Manchester Central	London St. Pancras	1.07pm	
1.05pm	SX	Eties	Rowsley	Ambergate	1.22pm	
12.20pm	SO	Exp	Cheadle Heath	London St. Pancras	1.19pm	
1.15pm	SO	Eties	Rowsley	Ambergate	1.32pm	
1.25pm	MX	Eties	Rowsley	Kirkby	1.42pm	Recessed High Peak Jn. for 12.20pm ex-Manchester.
12.20pm	EWD	Exp	Manchester Central	Nottingham	1.53pm	
1.50pm	EWD	Eties	Rowsley	Staveley	2.07pm	
1.25pm	EWD	Pass	Buxton	Derby	2.23pm	
1.15pm	MO	TF	Bakewell	Chaddesden	2.27pm	
11.50am	MX	Eties	Gowhole	Avenue	2.27pm	
12.10pm	EWD	ECS	Cornbrook Sidings	Derby	2.35pm	Attaches and detaches at stations enroute.

Time	Days	Type of train	From	To	Pass	Notes
2.20pm	MX	Eties	Rowsley	Kirkby	2.38pm	
2.30pm	EWD	Eties	Rowsley	Blackwell Sidings	2.47pm	Works at High Peak Junction.
1.50pm	EWD	Exp	Manchester Central	London St. Pancras	3.00pm	
2.10pm	SO	Exp	Chinley	Derby	3.09pm	
12.38pm	SX	Pass	Manchester Central	Derby	3.12pm	Held at Matlock for 16 minutes.
12.38pm	SO	Pass	Manchester Central	Derby	3.19pm	Held at Matlock for 23 minutes.
11.30am	SX Q	EF	Alexandra	Brent	3.25pm	
3.15pm	SO	EBV	Rowsley	Johnsons Sidings	3.28pm	
3.15pm	SX	Eties	Rowsley	Ambergate	3.32pm	
3.10pm	EWD	Exp	Buxton	Derby	3.49pm	
1.10pm	SO	Exp	Blackpool T. Rd	Derby	3.56pm	
3.55pm	SX	Min	Rowsley	Chaddesden	4.15pm	
12.00nn	EWD	Eties	Ashton Road	Kirkby	4.32pm	Regulated when 1.20pm Q ex Alexandra runs (below).
1.20pm	SX Q	EF	Alexandra	Brent	4.33pm	
3.58pm	SO Q	Exp	Chinley	Derby	4.51pm	
3.25pm	EWD	Exp	Manchester Central	Derby	5.00pm	
4.15pm	SX	Exp	Manchester Central	London St. Pancras	5.15pm	
5.18pm	EWD	Exp	Matlock	Nottingham	5.27pm	
4.20pm	EWD	Exp	Manchester Central	London St. Pancras	5.34pm	
5.30pm	EWD	EBV	Rowsley	High Peak Junction	5.42pm	
12.25pm	EWD	Eties	Cheadle Sidings	Staveley	5.45pm	
5.20pm	SO	Exp	Chinley	London St. Pancras	5.56pm	
4.37pm	EWD	Pass	Millers Dale	Derby	6.12pm	
4.45pm	SO	Exp	Manchester Central	Derby	6.32pm	
4.45pm	SX	Exp	Manchester Central	Derby	6.37pm	
3.25pm	SX Q	EF	Alexandra	West End Sidings	6.42pm	
5.50pm	EWD	Exp	Manchester Central	London St. Pancras	6.54pm	
6.54pm	SX	Pass	Rowsley	Derby	7.14pm	
5.52pm	SO	Pass	Buxton	Derby	7.14pm	Recessed on slow line at Darley Dale.
4.20pm	WThX	Exp	Blackpool T. Rd	Leicester	7.33pm	
7.15pm	WO	Exp	Rowsley	London St. Pancras	7.33pm	Standard excursion. Runs 1st July to 9th September.
7.05pm	EWD	Eties	Rowsley	Kirkby	7.48pm	Recessed at Matlock.
7.40pm	MO	Exp	Rowsley	Camp Hill	8.00pm	See Note 14
7.50pm	ThSO	Eties	Rowsley	Blackwell Sidings	8.10pm	
8.00pm	SO	Exp	Rowsley	Camp Hill	8.21pm	See Note 15
8.00pm	ThO	Exp	Rowsley	Sheffield	8.22pm	Standard excursion. Runs 2nd July to 10th September.
8.15pm	EWD	Eties	Rowsley	Ambergate	8.32pm	
8.25pm	ThSX	Eties	Rowsley	Blackwell Sidings	8.45pm	
8.33pm	SO	Min	Matlock	Chaddesden	8.46pm	
8.25pm	ThO	Pass	Rowsley	Nottingham	8.48pm	Standard excursion. Runs 2nd July to 10th September.
6.18pm	SO	Pass	Manchester Central	Derby	8.56pm	
7.25pm	SO	Exp	Manchester Central	Nottingham	9.03pm	
7.25pm	SX	Exp	Manchester Central	Nottingham	9.07pm	
6.18pm	SX	Pass	Manchester Central	Derby	9.18pm	
8.54pm	SO	Pass	Rowsley	Derby	9.18pm	
9.00pm	SO	Pass	Rowsley	Burton	9.26pm	See Note 16
9.10pm	EWD	Min	Rowsley	Chaddesden	9.30pm	See also entry below.
9.12pm	SO	Min	Rowsley	Chaddesden	9.32pm	Applies when 9.00pm standard excursion from Rowsley runs.
6.22pm	MO	Exp	Blackpool T. Rd	Leicester / Nottingham	9.50pm	See Note 17
9.35pm	EWD	Eties	Rowsley	Beeston	9.58pm	See Note 18
10.00pm	SX	EF	Rowsley	Derby	10.13pm	
10.15pm	SX	Eties	Rowsley	Toton	10.32pm	Regulated FO to follow 8.42pm Standard excursion from Manchester.
8.42pm	FO	Exp	Manchester Central	Derby	10.33pm	See Note 19

14 Standard excursion. Runs 6th July to 24th August (except 3rd August).

15 Standard excursion. Runs 4th & 11th July and 29th August, and as required.

16 Standard excursion. Runs 4th July to 5th September (except 1st and 8th August).

17 Standard excursion. Runs 6th July to 28th September (except 3rd August).

18 Regulated MO to follow 6.22pm standard excursion from Blackpool.

19 Standard excursion. Runs 3rd July to 18th September. Also conveys portion from Blackburn, depart 7.55pm.

Time	Days	Type of train	From	To	Pass	Notes
10.40pm	FO	Min	Matlock	Chaddesden	10.50pm	See Note 20
10.45pm	SX	Min	Matlock	Chaddesden	10.55pm	See also entry above.
10.03pm	MO	Exp	Cheadle Heath	Leicester / Nottingham	11.12pm	See Note 21
11.15pm	SX	EF	Rowsley	St. Pancras Goods	11.28pm	
11.35pm	EWD	Min	Matlock	Staveley	11.45pm	
7.40pm	SO	TF	Cheadle Sidings	Leicester	11.57pm	
Sundays						
11.45pm	SO	Min	Rowsley	Chaddesden	12.02am	
10.05pm	SO	EF	Ancoats	St. Pancras Goods	12.33am	
9.15pm	SO	EF	Ancoats	Lawley Street	12.59am	
12.01am	Sun	Exp	Manchester Central	London St. Pancras	1.25am	
11.32pm	SO	Exp	Liverpool Central	Derby	1.33am	
10.00pm	SO	Eties	Heaton Mersey	Blackwell Sidings	2.56am	
9.03pm	SO	TF	Huskisson	Burton	3.41am	
3.45am	Sun	TF	Rowsley	St. Pancras Goods	4.02am	
4.00am	Sun	TF	Rowsley	Saltley	4.17am	
9.35pm	SO	TF	Brunswick	Nottingham	4.37am	
5.30am	Sun	TF	Rowsley	Leicester	5.47am	
6.00am	Sun	TF	Rowsley	Chaddesden	6.21am	
9.00am	Sun	TF	Rowsley	Saltley	9.17am	
10.10am	Sun	Exp	Manchester Central	Derby	11.20am	
9.15am	Sun	Pass	Manchester Central	Derby	11.59am	
12.00nn	Sun	Exp	Manchester Central	London St. Pancras	1.13pm	
12.25pm	Sun	Exp	Manchester Central	London St. Pancras	1.45pm	
4.40pm	Sun	Exp	Manchester Central	Derby	6.14pm	
5.25pm	Sun	Exp	Manchester Central	London St. Pancras	6.34pm	
7.25pm	Sun	Pass	Rowsley	Derby	7.45pm	
7.40pm	Sun	Pass	Buxton	Derby	8.44pm	
6.05pm	Sun	Pass	Manchester Central	Derby	9.04pm	
10.40pm	Sun	Exp	Manchester Central	Derby	11.53pm	

Left: Long-time Station Master Walter Best is standing under the canopy on the Down platform as Compound No.925 emerges from Willersley Tunnel with an Up express on an unidentified day in August 1934. The engine, which is clearly working hard, is probably running late or has a heavy load. Smoke from the tunnel would follow the train and envelop parts of the station for a short while. [E.R. Morten]

Right: The classic view of Cromford Station. In contrast to the previous shot, Class 5X Jubilee No.45554 *Canada* appears to be coasting as it passes through the station with an Up express on 4th July 1953. The engine was allocated to Nottingham shed at that time. [E.R. Morten]

[20] Applies 3rd July to 25th September. Runs early to avoid clash at Ambergate with 8.45pm York to Bristol standard excursion.

[21] Standard excursion. Runs 13th July to 7th September (except 3rd August).

APPENDIX "G"
PASSENGER EXCURSION TRAINS TIMED TO PASS CROMFORD SIDINGS SIGNAL BOX BETWEEN MONDAY 13TH AND SUNDAY 19TH JULY 1914

[Times are estimated based on passing / arrival / departure times at adjacent locations]

DOWN LINE

Time	Days	From	To	Pass	Notes
Weekdays					
3.23am	SO	Sutton-in-Ashfield	Blackpool TR	4.11am	
2.00am	SO	Bedford	Blackpool TR	4.39am	
2.50am	SO	Basford	Blackpool TR	4.51am	
4.20am	SO	Burton	Blackpool TR	5.05am	Marston, Thompson & Evershed excursion.
3.45am	SO	Ashby	Blackpool TR	5.15am	Marston, Thompson & Evershed excursion.
3.54am	SO	Leicester	Blackpool TR	5.42am	Also conveys portion from Nottingham (dep 4.15am), attached at Trent.
5.33am	SO	Tibshelf	Southport	6.14am	South Normanton Band of Hope.
3.37am	SO	Wellingborough	Liverpool Central	6.55am	
4.48am	SO	Redditch	Blackpool TR	7.29am	
?	ThO	Coventry	Buxton	9.30am	Coventry departure time not shown; to MR at Wigston at 7.54am. (Coventry Co-op).
7.38am	WO	Camp Hill	Rowsley	10.07am	Standard excursion running on additional day.
12.50pm	ThO	Worksop	Buxton	2.10pm	
Sundays					
2.56am	Sun	Trent	Colne	3.36am	

UP LINE

Time	Days	From	To	Pass	Notes
Weekdays					
10.10pm	FO	Colne	St. Pancras	2.00am	At Cromford on Saturday morning.
10.45am	SO	Chinley	St. Pancras	11.17am	Relief to 10.15am Manchester Central to St. Pancras.
7.40pm	WO	Rowsley	Camp Hill	8.00pm	Standard excursion running on additional day.
8.26pm	ThO	Buxton	Worksop	9.22pm	
9.15pm	ThO	Buxton	Coventry	9.55pm	Coventry Co-op.
7.50pm	SO	Southport	Tibshelf	10.31pm	
Sundays					
9.30pm	SO	Blackpool TR	Bedford	12.56am	
9.55pm	SO	Blackpool TR	Redditch	1.04am	
10.55pm	SO	Liverpool Central	Wellingborough	1.16am	
10.35pm	SO	Blackpool TR	Leicester / Nottingham	2.02am	
10.57pm	SO	Blackpool TR	Basford / Sutton-in-A	2.20am	Trains combined on return.
11.10pm	SO	Blackpool TR	Burton	2.30am	Marston, Thompson & Evershed excursion.
11.30pm	SO	Blackpool TR	Ashby	2.41am	Marston, Thompson & Evershed excursion.

Note the early starts of the Blackpool excursions and the late departures from the resort, giving many of the passengers a 24-hour round trip. They certainly got good value for their money.

Compound No.1036 was built in November 1908 and was initially allocated to Leeds. By 1914 it had been transferred to Kentish Town and would be regularly seen working expresses through Cromford. This photo taken on 29th July 1948 shows the engine now allocated to Derby and in charge of an Up stopping train at Cromford. It did little work after this and was withdrawn from service in October of the same year without receiving its new BR number (41036).

[H.K. Boulter]

APPENDIX "H"

TRAINS CALLING AT CROMFORD STATION JULY, AUGUST AND SEPTEMBER 1914

With the exception of the standard excursions, the times shown are those for departures in the public timetable. These can be one or two minutes earlier than those in the working timetable from which the passing times at Cromford Sidings signal box have been determined. Most trains called for one minute, but some called for two minutes and one for three. The additional minutes were presumably for dealing with parcels traffic or milk churns rather than passengers. The minutes of calls of two and three minutes are shown in square brackets in the notes column.

Time	Days	From	To	Up Line	Down Line	Notes
Weekdays						
7.10am	EWD	Derby	Manchester Central		7.53am	[2]
7.33am	EWD	Bakewell	Derby	7.56am		Locally known as *'The Joe Wright'* after the guard who worked the train from 1886 to 1928.
8.19am	EWD	Millers Dale	Derby	8.57am		
9.45am	EWD	Derby	Manchester Central		10.22am	
10.06am	EWD	Buxton	Derby	10.55am		
11.25am	EWD	Buxton	Derby	12.30pm		
12.05pm	EWD	Derby	Buxton		1.06pm	
1.21pm	SX	Derby	Rowsley		2.02pm	[2]
1.21pm	SO	Derby	Buxton		2.02pm	[2]
1.10pm	SO	Burton	Rowsley		2.08pm	Standard excursion. Runs 4th July to 5th September (except 1st and 8th August).
1.25pm	ThO	Nottingham	Rowsley		2.22pm	Standard excursion. Runs 2nd July to 10th September.
1.26pm	ThO	Sheffield	Rowsley		2.32pm	Standard excursion. Runs 2nd July to 10th September.
12.38pm	SX	Manchester Central	Derby	3.11pm		
12.38pm	SO	Manchester Central	Derby	3.16pm		3.18pm in WTT.
3.43pm	EWD	Derby	Manchester Central		4.26pm	
3.58pm	SO Q	Chinley	Derby	4.50pm		Express. Duplicate of 4.59pm departure.
3.25pm	EWD	Manchester Central	Derby	4.59pm		Express
4.37pm	EWD	Millers Dale	Derby	6.10pm		[2]
6.18pm	TFX	Cromford	Manchester Victoria		6.18pm	Runs until 31st August. Express from Rowsley.
5.45pm	EWD	Derby	Rowsley		6.31pm	[2]
6.54pm	SX	Rowsley	Derby	7.11pm		
5.52pm	SO	Buxton	Derby	7.11pm		
7.20pm	EWD	Derby	Manchester Central		7.46pm	Express
8.00pm	ThO	Rowsley	Sheffield	8.21pm		Standard excursion. Runs 2nd July to 10th September.
8.25pm	ThO	Rowsley	Nottingham	8.47pm		Standard excursion. Runs 2nd July to 10th September.
6.18pm	SX	Manchester Central	Derby	9.16pm		
8.54pm	SO	Rowsley	Derby	9.16pm		
9.00pm	SO	Rowsley	Burton	9.25pm		Standard excursion. Runs 4th July to 5th September (except 1st and 8th August).
Sundays						
7.10am	Sun	Derby	Manchester Central		7.47am	[3]
10.20am	Sun	Derby	Rowsley		10.53am	
9.15am	Sun	Manchester Central	Derby	11.58am		
2.05pm	Sun	Derby	Buxton		2.38pm	
6.55pm	Sun	Derby	Manchester Central		7.32pm	
7.25pm	Sun	Rowsley	Derby	7.44pm		
7.40pm	Sun	Buxton	Derby	8.42pm		[2]
6.05pm	Sun	Manchester Central	Derby	9.02pm		

APPENDIX "I"
THE CROMFORD & DISTRICT BRANCH OF THE AMALGAMATED SOCIETY OF RAILWAY SERVANTS

The notebooks show that Charles Burling was an active member of the Cromford & District Branch of the National Union of Railwaymen. The union was constituted on 29th March 1913 by a combination of the Amalgamated Society of Railway Servants (formed 1872), The General Railway Workers' Union (1890) and the United Pointsmen's and Signalmen's Society (1880). It is not known which union Charles was a member of prior to the formation of the NUR.

The Cromford & District Branch was formed as a branch of the ASRS at a meeting held in the Greyhound Hotel, Cromford, on Sunday 3rd January 1897. Prior to that time the nearest branches were at Ambergate and Rowsley, neither of which were particularly convenient for those who worked at intermediate locations and wished to attend meetings. In fact, officers of the former branch chaired and spoke at the meeting to encourage the formation of a Cromford branch. Samuel Millington, a signalman, was appointed the first secretary – and was also the first person to register as a member.

The Cromford & District Branch catered for members who worked at Midland Railway locations between Whatstandwell and Matlock and those who were employed on the lower section of the London & North Western Railway's Cromford & High Peak line.

The balance sheet and supporting information for the year ending 31st December 1897 is reproduced below. Note that odd entries contained amounts involving farthings. These have been omitted for clarity:

BALANCE SHEET

Receipts			
Members Scale A – 5d per week		27. 1. 8	
Members Scale B – 3d per week		9. 5. 9	
			36. 7. 5
Collections for Orphan Fund			4. 0. 0
Sundries			5. 0
	Total		40.12. 5
Expenditure			
Donations and travelling benefit – Scale B		3.10. 0	
Suspension benefit – Scale B		1.16. 0	
			5. 6. 0
7/10th of members' contributions – Scale A		19. 4. 2	
Half of members' contributions – Scale B		4.12.10	
			23.17. 0
To Orphan Fund			4. 0. 0
Branch management:			
¾d for each members – Scale A		4. 1. 3	
¾d for each members – Scale B		2. 6. 5	
			6. 7. 8
Balance in hand			1. 1. 9
	Total		40.12. 5

BRANCH MANAGEMENT ACCOUNT

Receipts

Entrance fees – new members		3. 9. 0
From balance sheet (¾d per member)		6. 7. 8
Sale of rules, cards, etc.		2. 5.11
	Total	12. 2. 7

Expenditure

To branch secretary (⅓ allowed from contributions)		2. 2. 7
Rent of meeting room		2. 2. 0
Remittance to general office for goods supplied		2. 4. 6
Printing, postage, carriage of parcels		2.19. 0
Cash in treasurer's hands		2.14. 6
	Total	12. 2. 7

NUMBER OF MEMBERS

Number of members Dec. 1896	–	Members deceased	–
New members	69	Transferred to other branches	1
Transferred from other branches	2	Withdrawals	6
Total	71	Total	7
		Grand Total	66

It will be noted that the grand total should actually be 64 – or the withdrawals 4 – but these are the figures that were actually shown on the annual return!

PAYMENTS TO MEMBERS (for donation, suspension, allowance and travelling relief)

J. Poundall	Scale B	Platelayer	Cromford	3.10. 0
J. Jepson	Scale B	Hanger On	Cromford	1.16. 0

BRANCH OFFICIALS

Chairman	William Day	Matlock Bridge
Secretary	Samuel Millington	Cromford
Treasurer	Elijah Sheldon	Cromford
Trustees	Henry Spencer	Bonsall
	Richard Swinscoe	Cromford
	John Sheldon	Cromford
Auditors	Andrew Burdett	Matlock Bath
	James Vearnals	Matlock Bath

The public houses where the Cromford & District branch of the ASRS held its initial meetings – the Greyhound Hotel in Cromford Market Place and the Boat Inn in Scarthin. Meetings were also held at the Rutland Arms Hotel at Masson (see page 27).

Details of the original members and those who joined the union during 1897 are shown in Appendix "J". It will be noted that the statistics relating to members on page 55 do not wholly agree with information in that appendix. One significant feature is the number of men leaving the union after a short period of membership. The ASRS appears to have had a rather chequered history in this respect. Within a year of its formation, there were 17,247 members, but internal disputes resulted in the number falling back to just 6,300 in 1882. Recruitment drives in the following years increased the membership again, especially in the 1890s when the Cromford & District Branch was formed – it can be seen from Appendix "J" that this concentrated on certain grades. However, many did not see any immediate benefit from their union membership and ceased to pay their subscriptions. The number of members in Appendix "J" shown as leaving the union before the end of 1897 is significantly more than the end of the year statistics show. Those who were in arrears towards the end of the year were probably included in these statistics on the grounds that their overdue subs would be paid. If this was the case – and it can only be conjecture 110 years later – then the true significance was to be found in the return for 1898. The membership details were now:

Number of members Dec. 1897	66	Members deceased	1
New members	7	Transferred to other branches	2
Transferred from other branches	2	Withdrawals (incl. 3 'struck off')	41
Total	75	Total	44
		Grand Total	31

A number of the branch officials had also changed, including the chairman and secretary – who were now respectively T. Sanders of Whatstandwell, and John Fern of Bonsall.

In 1898, the union meetings were held at the Boat Inn in Scarthin, but they were later transferred to the Rutland Arms at Masson. By 1914 when Charles Burling had moved to the area – and the NUR had been formed – it was found that this venue was too small for those attending the meetings. Charles records that on 17th June of that year, the meetings were transferred to the Greyhound Hotel Reading Room at Cromford.

Charles came to Cromford in 1911. The membership statistics for that year were:

Number of members Dec. 1910	34	Members deceased	–
New members	7	Transferred to other branches	1
Transferred from other branches	1	Withdrawals	4
Total	42	Total	5
		Grand Total	37

The branch officials were:

Chairman	Edward Purslow	Matlock		
Vice Chairman	H. Butcher	Starkholmes		
Secretary	E. Ashman	Whatstandwell		
Treasurer	S. Bateman	Cromford		
Trustees	P. Higton	Middleton	J. Griffin	Whatstandwell
	A. Burdett	Matlock Bath		
Auditors	H. Bennett	Whatstandwell	G.H. Workman	Whatstandwell
Check Steward	J. Ellis	Matlock		

Of significance in the accounts was an honorary membership fee of 10s.6d from C.F. White and a payment of 2s.6d *'unjust fine Bro. Purslow'* – the chairman of the branch. This may have been associated with the 1911 national strike, for which there was an expenditure of £1.17s.0d.

The last records as an ASRS branch – for 1912 – show that membership had risen to 42. Unfortunately, similar records do not appear to have survived for the early NUR period, so we cannot say whether Charles became one of the branch officials. However, he does tell us that at the end of 1913 the number of branch members had increased to 89 – more than double the situation at the end of the previous year. While there would be new recruits, some, no doubt, would have come from the other unions.

The increase in the number of members eventually led to the formation of a new branch at Matlock at the end of October 1915. The initial membership was 37, comprising 26 transfers from the Cromford Branch and 11 new.

Appendix "J"

MEMBERS OF THE CROMFORD & DISTRICT BRANCH OF THE ASRS DURING ITS FIRST YEAR – 1897

See Appendix "I" for notes about the formation of the branch. It should be pointed out that the registration books kept by the ASRS – which were passed to the NUR and subsequently endorsed as appropriate – were initially compiled in 1897. Additions appear to have been entered on a monthly basis, though it is clear that odd entries were made at a later stage / out of sequence. Many exclusion dates also appear to have been made retrospectively – especially those that applied to the first year. Otherwise, the year end return of members would have produced a completely different figure. There are two cases where the joining and exclusion date are the same. It is possible, of course that these men registered but did not pay any subscriptions.

No.	Surname	Forename	Age	Grade	Company	Joined	Retired	Died	Excluded	Comment
51877	Millington	Samuel	36	Signalman	Midland	03.01.1897			09.1928	The first branch secretary. To Stockport No.1 branch 03.12.1906; back to Cromford branch 16.09.1907. Involved in accident 10.02.1909.
51878	Roe	J.D.	28	Signalman	Midland	03.01.1897	05.09.1934			To Rowsley branch 17.09.1897; back to Cromford branch 09.01.1899, then to new Matlock branch 27.10.1915.
51879	Bateman	Samuel	45	Ganger	Midland	03.01.1897		02.1933		See Appendix "R"
51880	Sheldon	Elijah	38	Engine Driver	L&NW	03.01.1897			30.06.1902	The first branch treasurer. Excluded due to subscription arrears.
51881	Jepson	James	34	Hanger On	L&NW	03.01.1897			30.09.1898	Excluded due to subscription arrears.
51882	Marples	Arthur	30	Under Ganger	Midland	03.01.1897			31.12.1899	Excluded due to subscription arrears.
51883	Hemson	G.	30	Signalman	Midland	03.01.1897	10.03.1931	31.01.1944		To Peak Dale branch 13.12.1898; to Buxton branch 16.06.1902; to New Mills branch 01.01.1908.
51884	Swinscoe	Richard	40	Platelayer	Midland	03.01.1897		01.03.1904		A trustee of the branch during its first year.
51885	Gould	W.	28	Signalman	Midland	03.01.1897			31.12.1898	Excluded due to subscription arrears.
51886	Burdett	Andrew J.	33	Signalman	Midland	03.01.1897			31.12.1899	An auditor of the branch during its first year. Excluded due to subscription arrears.
51887	Haines	J.H.	33	Drayman	Midland	03.01.1897			30.09.1898	Excluded due to subscription arrears.
51888	Taylor	William	32	Drayman	Midland	03.01.1897			30.09.1898	Excluded due to subscription arrears.
51889	Lee	B.	46	Foreman	Midland	03.01.1897		03.1922		
51890	Vearnals	James	41	Station Porter	Midland	03.01.1897			25.04.1897	No reason given for exclusion. Exclusion date either incorrect or rejoined, as Vearnals was shown as an auditor in the 1897 year end statistics.
51891	Lee	Joseph A.	24	Platelayer	Midland	03.01.1897				
51892	Sheldon	John	53	Fireman	L&NW	03.01.1897			30.06.1899	A trustee of the branch during its first year. Excluded due to subscription arrears.
51893	Spencer	Henry	24	Platelayer	Midland	03.01.1897			31.03.1901	A trustee of the branch during its first year. No reason given for exclusion.
51894	Griffin	James	40	Platelayer	Midland	03.01.1897				

No.	Surname	Forename	Age	Grade	Company	Joined	Retired	Died	Excluded	Comment
51895	Allcock	W.	23	Station Porter	Midland	10.01.1897			see note	To unidentified branch 16.10.1898, then to Rowsley branch at an unspecifield date. Shown as excluded due to subscription arrears 21.12.1900.
51896	Simmons	George	19	Porter	Midland	30.01.1897			02.01.1898	No reason given for exclusion.
51897	Workman	Charles	20	Machine Youth	Midland	10.01.1897			27.06.1897	No reason given for exclusion.
51898	Greenhough	Charles	57	Platelayer	Midland	19.01.1897			30.11.1897	Excluded due to subscription arrears.
53767	Hill	John Thomas	31	Drayman	Midland	31.01.1897		10.10.1898		
53768	Ellis	James	38	Drayman	Midland	31.01.1897			30.06.1901	Excluded due to subscription arrears.
53769	Bonsall	John	18	Parcels Carman	Midland	31.01.1897				
53770	Tombs	Arthur	23	Drayman	Midland	31.01.1897			30.06.1901	Excluded due to subscription arrears.
53771	Allen	Walter	39	Drayman	Midland	31.01.1897			30.11.1897	Excluded due to subscription arrears.
53772	Allen	Richard	40	Drayman	Midland	31.01.1897			21.11.1897	No reason given for exclusion.
53773	Poultney	William H.	25	Drayman	Midland	31.01.1897			31.10.1897	No reason given for exclusion.
53774	Birch	Harry	23	Drayman	Midland	31.01.1897			30.06.1901	Excluded due to subscription arrears.
62463	Slack	John	34	Fireman	L&NW	14.03.1897			30.06.1899	Excluded due to subscription arrears.
62464	Higton	Paul	48	Breaksman	L&NW	14.03.1897	31.05.1917	23.11.1917		
62465	Clifford	T.	25	Signalman	Midland	14.03.1897			12.12.1897	No reason given for exclusion.
62466	Neale	Charles	28	Signalman	Midland	14.03.1897			21.11.1897	No reason given for exclusion.
65549	Gould	Job	24	Fireman	L&NW	04.04.1897			19.09.1897	Excluded due to subscription arrears.
65550	Warrington	William	47	Ganger	L&NW	04.04.1897			08.08.1897	No reason given for exclusion.
65551	Baker	Edward	28	Signalman	L&NW	04.04.1897			03.1932	Excluded due to subscription arrears.
65552	Swindell	Samuel	23	Platelayer	L&NW	04.04.1897			08.08.1897	Excluded due to subscription arrears.
65553	Gregory	John	35	Platelayer	L&NW	04.04.1897			08.08.1897	Excluded due to subscription arrears.
65554	Statham	Frederick	31	Platelayer	Midland	04.04.1897			31.03.1900	Excluded due to subscription arrears.
65555	Keightley	Gerald	20	Labourer	Midland	04.04.1897			30.09.1898	Excluded due to subscription arrears.
65556	Wilburn	Henry	27	Labourer	Midland	04.04.1897			31.12.1899	Excluded due to subscription arrears.
65557	Crooks	John	35	Labourer	Midland	04.04.1897			30.09.1898	Excluded due to subscription arrears. Surname could be Crooke.
70150	Poundall	J.	51	Platelayer	Midland	25.04.1897			30.09.1904	Excluded due to subscription arrears.
70151	Spencer	Joseph A.	20	Cleaner	L&NW	25.04.1897			30.06.1901	Excluded due to subscription arrears.
74144	Hallows	Ralph A.	20	Platelayer	L&NW	15.04.1897			21.11.1897	Excluded due to subscription arrears.
74145	Slack	Henry	50	Platelayer	L&NW	15.04.1897			08.08.1897	Excluded due to subscription arrears.
74146	Cooper	John	64	Platelayer	L&NW	15.04.1897			08.08.1897	Excluded due to subscription arrears.
74147	Prince	Frederick	33	Platelayer	Midland	06.06.1897			31.03.1901	Excluded due to subscription arrears.
75951	Skuce	F.W.	26	Signalman	Midland	27.06.1897			30.09.1902	To Peak Dale branch 11.12.1899. Excluded due to subscription arrears.
79378	Brown	Joseph	43	Platelayer	L&NW	18.07.1897			29.08.1897	No reason given for exclusion.
79379	Smith	James	34	Pointsman	L&NW	18.07.1897			17.10.1897	No reason given for exclusion.
79380	Higton	Job	43	Platelayer	L&NW	18.07.1897			18.07.1897	No reason given for exclusion. Joining and exclusion dates are the same.

82302	Taylor	George A.	33	Checker	Midland	08.08.1897		16.01.1898	Excluded due to subscription arrears.
85774	Massey	Andrew	34	Platelayer	Midland	19.09.1897		21.11.1897	Excluded due to subscription arrears.
85775	Massey	Henry	36	Ganger	Midland	19.09.1897		11.01.1907	Excluded due to subscription arrears.
85776	Massey	William	60	Ganger	Midland	19.09.1897	11.01.1906		
85777	Boden	William	32	Platelayer	Midland	19.09.1897		17.10.1897	Excluded due to subscription arrears. Died as the result of an accident 19.11.1912. See Appendix "E".
85778	Beech	Isaac	60	Platelayer	Midland	19.09.1897		17.10.1897	Excluded due to subscription arrears.
85779	Smedley	Samuel	60	Platelayer	Midland	19.09.1897		31.12.1905	Excluded due to subscription arrears.
85780	Hood	Mark	27	Signalman	Midland	19.09.1897		31.10.1897	Excluded due to subscription arrears.
85781	Sweeting	John William	30	Platelayer	Midland	19.09.1897		30.09.1898	Excluded due to subscription arrears.
85782	Fern	John	35	Ganger	Midland	19.09.1897	10.1922		
91692	Willacy	John Henry	22	Drayman	Midland	17.10.1897		31.10.1907	No reason given for exclusion.
91693	Thurlow	Frank	20	Drayman	Midland	17.10.1897		31.10.1907	No reason given for exclusion.
91694	Mawson	William James	18	Booking Clerk	Midland	17.10.1897		30.09.1898	Excluded due to subscription arrears.
94779	Eite	Samuel	34	Platelayer	Midland	31.10.1897		30.09.1898	Excluded due to subscription arrears.
94780	Purslow	Edward	25	Drayman	Midland	31.10.1897			
97270	Shaw	William	24	Drayman	Midland	21.11.1897		21.11.1897	No reason given for exclusion. Joining and exclusion dates are the same.

Transferred In

21385	Day	R. William	25	Signalman	Midland	25.01.1893	31.12.1907

A member of Rowsley branch on joining the union. Shown as transferred to the Cromford branch on 27.12.1896. As this date is slightly earlier than the one quoted for new members, he can be said to have been the first member of the branch. Became the first Chairman.

The year end statistics for 1897 show that another person was transferred in during the year. Unfortunately, he has not been identified.

Members of the Cromford & District Branch of the ASRS / NUR were employed at a number of locations, operated by both the Midland and London & North Western Railways. Illustrated here are shots of Whatstandwell station, Midland Railway – which also had station signals like Cromford, though worked a little differently – and Cromford Goods on the L&NW's Cromford & High Peak section.

APPENDIX "K"
DERAILMENT OF GOODS TRAIN AT CHURCH LANE CROSSING, DARLEY DALE, ON FRIDAY 19TH SEPTEMBER 1913

As was the practice in those days, the *High Peak News* for Saturday 27th September 1913 included a rather detailed account of this incident, although it did not mention Church Lane Crossing specifically. Instead, it referred to a location *'about 500 yards above Darley Dale station'* where *'several trucks were upset and blocked both up and down lines'*. It went on to say that the breakdown gang from Rowsley Shed[1] were soon on the scene and the work of clearing the trucks proceeded quickly.

However, the 7.25pm express from Manchester to Nottingham, which was due at Matlock at 8.53pm was held on the Rowsley side of the blockage, as was the 6.35pm slow passenger train from Manchester, due Darley Dale at 8.42pm[2]. On the Down side at Matlock was what was referred to as *'the slow passenger from there to Darley due to leave at 8.40pm'*. This, in fact, was 8.15pm Derby to Buxton, due to depart at 8.49pm. This train must have been shunted out of the way, as the 5.35pm express from St. Pancras to Manchester, which was due from Matlock at 8.54pm and to pass the slow train between Darley Dale station and Church Lane Crossing, came as far as Matlock to set down passengers for the town. An engine was then attached to the other end (possibly the inwards train loco), and the train then proceeded to Manchester via Ambergate, Chesterfield, and the Dore & Chinley line.

The Down line was the first to be cleared and the *'slow passenger'* to Manchester left Matlock at 10.20pm. The 7.25pm express from Manchester did not arrive at Matlock until shortly before 11.0pm – around 2 hours late – followed by the slow passenger train from Manchester. One inhabitant of Bakewell, who was held up at Matlock by the delay was reported as having *'a motor-car from the Matlock station to get home'*.

An Up express approaches Church Lane Crossing in 1913. The pedestrian bridge was erected in 1911.

[1] Situated near the station in the vicinity of the new Peak Village complex. The later engine shed, being developed by Peak Rail, was not opened until 1926.

[2] The train was in fact the 6.18pm from Manchester Central via Marple. It was probably referred to as the 6.35pm departure, as passengers could leave Manchester at that time on a service to Buxton via Cheadle Heath and change into the 6.18pm departure at Chinley, where there was a 10 minute connection. The service itself ran to Matlock. The public timetable indicates that after the passengers had alighted, the stock was shunted clear for the 7.25pm express from Manchester, and then returned to the station to form a 9.8pm all stations service from Matlock to Derby.

Appendix "L"

CROMFORD STATION MASTERS

Passenger services between Ambergate and Rowsley were introduced on 4th June 1849. Cromford station had not been completed at that time, but had opened by early July. The Station Master's house was a later structure, which is believed to have been designed by Paxton's son-in-law, G.H. Stokes, and was built in 1855.

Name	To Cromford	From Cromford	Comment
Anthill William Lee(s)	1849	by 1856	Shown as Anthill William Lees in 1850 Slater's Directory. In 1851 census shown as William Lee, aged 39, born Beeley, living with his wife at Masson House, Matlock Bath.
Edwin Furniss	by 1856	Retired 1881?	In 1861 census shown as aged 45, born Pilsley, living in the Station House at Cromford with his wife Sarah (29) and 3 children – one (aged 8) born at Stanton and two (aged 3 and 1) at Matlock. They had two other children in later years. Two of the family – Laurence and Charles – were later shown as railway clerks. In the 1881 census he was aged 65. In 1891 he was shown as retired and living in Scarthin. It is possible that he was transferred to Cromford when the Station Master's house was built in 1855.
Richard Joseph Oram	By January 1882	After January 1888	
Lewis Wright	by April 1891	by 1894	In 1891 census shown as aged 32, born Darley Dale, living with his wife Amelia and 4 children.
Harry I'Anson	by 1894	by January 1900	Possibly transferred to Chinley. Later at Bakewell, and at Matlock from April 1913.
Hedley V. Weston	by January 1900	After April 1901	In 1901 census shown as aged 36, born Horsley Woodhouse, living with his wife Mary (39) and son John (6). Transferred to Cheadle Heath in 1901.
Joseph Garibaldi Goss	by January 1903	by 1907	Transferred to SM Bamford.
Thomas Cooper	by 1907	13th October 1913	Transferred to SM Belle Vue.
William Brown	8th October 1913	by January 1922	From SM Buckden.
Walter Best	by January 1922	1938 or later	It would appear that the SM's post was a vacancy for quite some time after Walter Best left and was covered by a series of relief men. One – Reg Lowe – is known to have lived in a caravan in the front of the station: his wife became a porter during that period.
Harry Huntingdon	by 1950	by 1959	One time signalman Rowsley. To SM Wennington.
Alf Armitage	by 1959	c.1964	From SM Friden; to SM Harlington. Alf Armitage was the (blameless) signalman in the fatal crash at Harrow & Wealdstone in 1952.
J. G. McCulloch	c.1964	early 1967	From New Luce. To post in Glasgow area.

Taken on the same day as the cover photo – 15th June 1911 – again from a period postcard, we see Trafford Park Class 3 4-4-0 No.705 passing through the station on another Up express. This time Station Master Cooper is on the Down platform in discussion with another passenger, while two porters stand by a trolley of parcels on the Down side. The fact that no-one is looking at the train shows the posed nature of the photograph.

APPENDIX "M"
THE DEATH OF SIGNAL FITTER FREDERICK ELEY IN DOVE HOLES TUNNEL, FRIDAY 31ST OCTOBER 1913

At 2.40am on Saturday 1st November 1913, Peak Forest Station Master Charles James Waters was awakened from his sleep by ganger Thomas Turner to advise him that Turner had earlier received information from an engine driver of a body lying some 40 yards inside Dove Holes Tunnel at the Peak Forest end.

On receiving this advice, Turner had at once proceeded inside the tunnel and found the body of a man facing towards Peak Forest with his head underneath him near the Down side tunnel wall and his feet near the rails. When the body was turned over it was noted that his neck was dislocated. A doctor found that his skull was also fractured.

The body was identified as that of Frederick Eley of 31 Lime Grove, Romiley, a signal lock fitter aged 42. His wife Annie said that he had left home during the day for New Mills and was expected home at 5.45pm. However, he appears instead to have gone to Millers Dale to purchase eggs and grapes for his children who were ill. This was deduced from the fact that when the 5.26pm train from Millers Dale arrived at Chinley at 5.43pm[1] Inspector Albert Martin found Eley's tools, along with eggs and grapes, in a compartment of a 3rd class carriage in the centre of the train. Both doors were closed, but the window of one was open. There had been no time for anyone to alight from the compartment before Martin saw the articles. Martin then phoned Millers Dale station, but no-one remembered seeing a passenger carrying such items. George Cooper of Fairfield, Buxton, the guard on the train, said that it ran non-stop from Millers Dale and was *'a large train with around 50 people on it'*.

Thomas Turner later inspected the tunnel and found a newly chipped insulator. Insulators and bobbins, which were linked by wire, were situated along the tunnel walls about 10 feet from rail level, the purpose being to give alarm if the wire broke through a rock fall or similar occurrence – which had happened on occasions in the past.

There were marks on the side of the tunnel wall where soot had been removed. These extended for 4 or 5 yards on either side of the broken insulator and went gradually down towards rail level. However, the wire along the tunnel wall was not broken. The space between the carriage and the insulator was said to be 3 feet 10 inches.

At the subsequent inquest, the coroner stated that it was unlikely that more information would be found. The cause of death was clearly due to the deceased coming into contact with the side of the tunnel, but it was unclear how and why this happened. It seemed impossible if the tunnel wall was 3 feet 10 inches from the side of the carriage for Eley's head to come into contact with the tunnel wall. The body had first touched the tunnel wall and then the insulator. While it was possible that he was outside the carriage on the footboard, it could hardly be supposed that he wished to commit suicide in this way, and it was very unlikely that he was thrown out.

Dove Holes Tunnel from the south (Peak Forest) end. Frederick Eley met his untimely death a few yards inside the tunnel.

The jury decided that there was no evidence to prove that this was an accident and that the case should be left open. The verdict was *'deceased was found dead in the tunnel, but there was not sufficient evidence to show how he met his injuries'*.

Mrs Eley said that there was no reason for her husband to commit suicide. However, his death had left her *'in a sad position'*. Her family could not help her and her children were ill, while she was not strong herself. The jury decided to hand their fees to Mrs Eley to help her in her plight.

[1] The train was the 3.43pm from Derby to Chinley, which called at all stations to Millers Dale, and then ran non-stop to Chinley.

APPENDIX "N"
THE DEATH OF GANGER SAMUEL SMITH IN MILFORD TUNNEL, TUESDAY 16TH DECEMBER 1913

Yet another tunnel fatality occurred on Tuesday 16th December, this time in Milford Tunnel between Belper and Duffield. The victim was 54-year old ganger Samuel Smith, who lived at Castle Orchard, Duffield.

At the coroner's enquiry on Thursday 18th December, Alfred Clarke of 138 Shaftsbury Crescent, Derby, said that he was driving a goods engine with a brakevan through the tunnel at about 25mph when he struck something. He stopped and informed a number of platelayers further in the tunnel. He added that there was smoke in the tunnel and that a train was passing on the opposite line. He whistled as he entered the tunnel but the sound could have been drowned by the passing train.

Platelayer Frank Goodwin of Wirksworth Road, Duffield, said that Smith was the foreman of a gang of six. He was a careful and experienced man whom he had known for 25 years. The deceased had been examining the line on his own and had left Goodwin in charge of the other men. After being alerted by the engine driver, he found Smith clear of the rails in a space of about 2 feet between the rails and the tunnel wall. It was apparent that he had been struck when he was tightening a bolt with a spanner.

When examined by the doctor, Smith was found to have a fractured skull and was bleeding from the ears, nose and mouth. He died while being conveyed on a train out of the tunnel.

The jury returned a verdict of *'accidental death'*. They also expressed the opinion that engine whistles should be sounded more frequently, but Mr Walls of the NUR said that too much whistling would be confusing.

It was later revealed that a brother of the deceased – also a ganger – had been seriously injured in almost the same spot two years previously, and that Smith had taken his place! Their father, who was himself a platelayer, had been killed in the same vicinity some years earlier.

The south end of Milford Tunnel c.1910. The signalbox was opened on 16th May 1897 on the completion of the Down Goods line from Duffield. The commencement of the Up Goods Line between the two locations can be seen in the left foreground. This opened on 14th June of the same year.

APPENDIX "O"
THE TRAGIC DEATH OF PORTER JOSEPH PICKERING AT CROMFORD STATION ON 21ST FEBRUARY 1914

At 6.45pm on the evening of Saturday 21st February, Station Master William Brown went off duty leaving 49 year old porter Joseph Pickering in charge. Shortly before 7.0pm there was an explosion and fire broke out in the combined Station Master's / Booking Office.

It was customary on Saturday evenings for the late shift porter to wash the floor. On this occasion, however, it appears that instead of using water, Joseph Pickering was cleaning the floor with naptha. Possibly the presence of the office coal fire caused it to ignite and set part of the room on fire. Unfortunately, the force of the blast shut the office door, which had a fixed automatic lock, and trapped him inside amongst the flames. When the door was closed, a key had to be used to open it from both the inside and outside.

Thomas Marples of Lea Hall Farm was just arriving at the station with some milk churns and together with Harry Bush, William Worthy and another passenger who were waiting for a train attempted to open the office door. This was found to be impossible, so Marples rushed over the line to the Station Master's house. After finishing his duty, William Brown had gone into the village, but fortunately Mrs Brown was at home and had a key for the office.

When the door was opened it was not possible to get inside immediately due to the dense smoke, but when this was clear the first thing Marples encountered was a burning mop. This, in fact, provided sufficient light for them to see Pickering standing in a corner near the fireplace with his clothes in flames. Marples and Mrs Brown dragged him outside and stripped off the burning clothes. He was found to be semi-conscious, but with terrible burns to his head, face, arms and legs.

Joseph Pickering from a photograph that appeared in the *High Peak News*.

Mrs Brown – who was later commended for her bravery – helped to extinguish most of the flames with buckets of water before the Matlock Fire Brigade arrived. In the meantime, Marples and other waiting passengers got Pickering across to the Up platform and placed him in the guard's van of the 7.11pm departure to Derby (5.52pm ex Buxton), from where he was then taken to the Derbyshire Royal Infirmary. He was accompanied by porters Peter Brindley from Matlock Bath and Frederick Gibbs from Matlock, who had been sent on the train from their respective stations. They had no first aid equipment, but fortunately there was a nurse on the train. She too had no bandages, but tore up two aprons and used them to make the semi-conscious porter more comfortable. Even so, it must have been an agonisingly slow journey. The train was liberally timed, stopping at all stations, and was not scheduled to arrive at Derby until 7.52pm.

Unfortunately, Pickering's burns were so serious that he died just before midnight. He was a married man and lived at 76 Wirksworth Road, Cromford with his wife Dinah. He was the son of the late schoolmaster of Kirk Ireton, and for 9 years worked as a coachman to Dr Webb of Wirksworth. He then joined the Midland Railway as a porter at Matlock Bath, being later transferred to Cromford. He had worked for the Company for 23 years[1]. He had four grown up daughters and a son, John, who also worked for the Midland Railway, in his case at Millers Dale. His brother, a Timber Inspector for the Midland Railway at Derby had seen him the previous day when *'he was in the usual health'* and again in the Infirmary just before he died.

When William Brown returned to the station, after being informed of the incident by his daughter, he immediately telephoned Derby station and asked for an ambulance to meet the train. He found most of the office covered with dirt and water, though the majority of documents and the tickets were still intact. On further investigation he noticed that one part of the office ceiling had been blown about 4 inches out of place and one window was broken, apparently when the explosion occurred. The paintwork was blistered. It was later estimated that the repairs would cost £10.

Brown said that Pickering was always a sober and steady man. He had never known the deceased or any other porter use naptha before. A tank of naptha was kept around 160 yards from the Booking Office and was for the use of platelayers. However, Pickering had a key to the tank and could have obtained some if desired.

On 25th February, the day of the funeral, Joseph Pickering's coffin was brought to Cromford station on the 12.5pm train from Derby. Here it was met by numerous railway friends and officials from nearby stations. The names of the bearers are recorded on page 26.

The jury at the Coroner's inquest on the following day returned a verdict of *'accidental death'*.

[1] As reported in the *High Peak News*. In the 1901 census he was shown as a *'Rail Signalman, Tel Clk'*, aged 39. The newspaper was quite specific about his age at the time of the accident stating that he had celebrated his 49th birthday in the previous December.

Although Cromford station was de-staffed on 1st January 1968, it is still possible today to identify the door to the Booking / Station Master's Office. This particular photo – on which the door is identified by an arrow – was taken on 13th June 1970. [See also back cover]

[M.A. King]

APPENDIX "P"

THE DEATH OF JUNIOR PORTER DONALD PREECE NEAR CHURCH LANE CROSSING, FRIDAY 19TH MARCH 1915

Donald Preece was a 14-year old lad who lived with his parents at East Lodge, Stancliffe. He had been employed by the Midland Railway as a Junior Porter at Darley Dale station for about 7 months.

At around 2.10pm on the afternoon of Friday 19th March, Jesse Giddes of 4 Derwent View, Green Lane, an engine driver for the Stancliffe Estates Company, noticed a body at the side of the line, which *'was just alive'*. He at once informed signalman Robert Withers in Church Lane Crossing signal box some 30 to 40 yards away, who identified the body as that of Donald Preece, and then sent a message to the Station Master.

A coroner's inquest was held at Darley Dale station on the following afternoon. The body of the deceased was available for viewing in the waiting room.

Preece had been trained in his duties by George Wall, also a Junior Porter, who was aged 16 and had been employed by the Midland Railway for a couple of months longer than Preece. Their duties including the changing of signal lamps at Church Lane Crossing, which was done twice a week. Wall said Preece had not undertaken this work on his own until 4 weeks previously. Since that time the lads had taken it in turns to do the lamping, so the deceased had covered the duty on four occasions. To do this they walked along the side of the Up lines, facing the traffic, and then crossed over all lines near Church Lane Crossing box, where the oil and lamps were kept.

Joseph Lionel Woodcroft, a relief Station Master working at Darley Dale station at the time, said that he had last seen Preece before he had taken his dinner. At about 2.30pm he was contacted by signalman Robert Withers, who advised him that Preece had been knocked down near Church Lane Crossing and went straight to the spot. The driver and fireman of the Stancliffe Estates engine were there, as well as two platelayers. The body had not been touched, but it was quite evident that Preece was dead. He was lying on his side between the Up main and Up slow lines, nearest to the latter, with his head towards Rowsley. The width between the two lines at that point was about 8 feet.

Woodcroft said that the deceased *'would leave about 1.56pm'*[1] to do the lamping work. The last train to pass before the body was discovered was the 1.25pm from Buxton to Derby, which would have been at the spot where he was found at about 2.7pm. It was presumed that Preece had been hit by this train, although there was nothing on the line to indicate where this had happened.

[1] It is not known why such a precise time was quoted, unless it was an assessment on how long it would have taken Preece to get to the point where he was knocked down. It was not associated with a departure for lamping duties after attending to a train at Darley Dale station. The last trains booked to call at Darley Dale were at 12.17pm on the Up (Derby direction) and 1.19pm on the Down. There was a northbound train which departed from Matlock at 1.40pm, but this was not scheduled to call at Darley Dale – unless such a stop had been added in a supplement to the timetable. In any case, it would appear that Preece's presence at the station was not necessary, as the train that allegedly knocked him down was the next one to call there.

Asked by a juror on the training Preece had received and when he started to cover the lamping duties, Woodcroft said that as a relief man he could not answer this specifically, but Preece would have had a copy of the rules, which stated that you must not place yourself in danger. It was also asked if it was normal practice to employ boys of 14 on lamp duties. Arthur Snow, the District Controller at Rowsley, said that there was no rule that would forbid him doing such work. Boys of this age had always been employed on the railway, but there were now more than in previous years due to the war.

Remarking on the fact that Jesses Giddes had said that when he found the body Preece *'was just alive'*, the coroner asked if anyone had examined him. Neither Giddes, his fireman, nor the two platelayers had received any first aid training and did not know what to do. The coroner said that the sooner they took such a course the better.

Signalman Robert Withers, who because of his signalling duties, and need to contact Relief Station Master Woodcroft, did not stay at the scene after identifying Preece, said that he noticed a flicker of life, but that was all. He had not examined the body as there was a big wound on Preece's head about 2½ inches deep and that in his opinion he was practically dead. The coroner agreed that the wound on the head made the situation hopeless.

The coroner also felt that Preece had been knocked down in a different place from where he was found and would have been carried some distance by the train. He thought he would have been crossing the line when hit. Arthur Snow said that neither the driver nor the fireman of the 1.25pm from Buxton saw or heard anything.

Doctor Lawrence Abel Mackenzie of the Royal Army Medical Corps, stationed at Darley Dale, said that he was called to the scene and found a hole in the head of the deceased and the thigh cut. The injury to his head was sufficient to cause instantaneous death. He also remarked that men of the RAMC were drilling in the park next to the railway and thought that the deceased had stopped to look at them and did not hear the train approaching[2].

In summing up, the coroner said that there was a clear view in front of where the deceased was found and that he knew of the train. Preece should have been more alert, but boys of 14 did not exactly act in the same way as men of 24. The jury returned a verdict of *'accidental death'*. However, the foreman said that they felt that boys of 14 were far too young to perform such duties. If this was necessary, then they should be properly instructed by experienced men and not take instructions from boys about their own age. This recommendation would be passed to the Home Office for consideration.

Left: Although not the best of photos, this one taken from the Church Lane Crossing footbridge in LMS days shows the line to Stancliffe Quarry veering away to the left. It would be somewhere in the vicinity of this junction where Donald Preece was found. **Right:** Church Lane Crossing signalbox from the level crossing, with Class 3F No.43250 on a trip from Darley Dale to Rowsley Sidings, Donald Preece's body would have been found on the left of the photograph at a point between the train's breakvan and the two stop signals in the distance. [Author's collection / Gordon Coltas]

[2] Charles records in his notebook the arrival of over 1,000 men at Darley Dale on the 8th and 16th March 1915. He does not mention the RAMC – or any regiment – specifically, but it would appear from the above that they formed at least part of the contingent.

APPENDIX "Q"
FATAL ACCIDENT TO STONE MERCHANT JOHN SIMS NEAR WHATSTANDWELL ON SATURDAY 5TH JUNE 1915

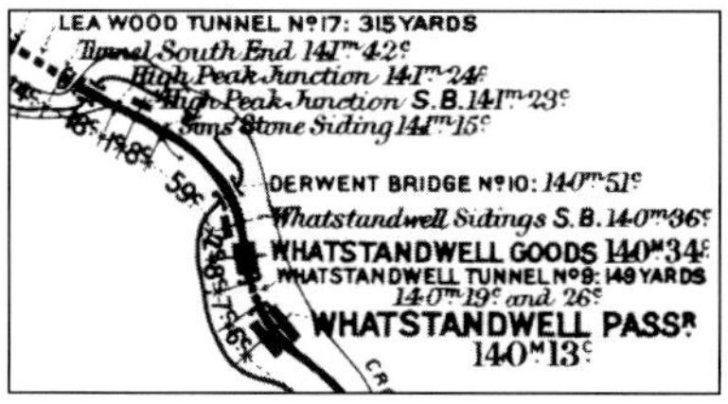

Forty-nine year old John Sims was a stone merchant at Whatstandwell and from a family with long associations with stone quarries. He was well respected in the area having been the Chairman of Crich Parish Council, and a member of the Belper Board of Guardians. For some 20 years he had walked along the railway line to get to and from his premises and had a permit from the Midland Railway for this purpose.

His brother, who last saw him alive at 9.0am on the previous morning, said that he was slightly deaf. The accident occurred near Bridge No.10, which was about half a mile north of Whatstandwell station, and where there was *'a slight curvature of the line'*. The direction in which Sims was walking indicates that he may have lived around the Homesford / High Peak Junction area.

Edward Harley, a bridge painter from Ambergate, was working on Bridge No.10 over the River Derwent near Dawbarn's Wood Works when he noticed something in the four foot. On investigation, he found John Sims' body doubled up and *'quite dead'*. He immediately proceeded towards Whatstandwell to advise Station Master William Hewitt of the circumstances.

In his submission at the subsequent coroner's inquest, Hewitt said that the driver of engine No.1021[1] hauling a slow train from Manchester[2] had informed him that he had noticed a hard hat blow by the side of his engine at that point, and asked Hewitt to search the line as he may have knocked someone down. Hewitt then proceeded down the line and met Harley coming towards him.

A verdict of *'accidental death'* was returned by the Coroner's jury.

APPENDIX "R"
A CYCLING ACCIDENT ON CROMFORD HILL INVOLVING SHUNTER JOHN WARD OF MATLOCK – 21ST JUNE 1915

At 5.40am on Monday 21st June, 23 year old John Ward left his home at 27 Steeple Grange, Bolehill, to cycle to Matlock station where he worked as a shunter. The first part of his journey was down the steep and winding Cromford Hill. He was coming round a corner near George Clemence Gould's shop when he collided with Samuel Bateman, a Midland Railway ganger, and was thrown from his bike.

Several people were soon on the scene to help. A man named Barber, who worked for Williams of Matlock Bath, and had been on a motor mail trip to Wirksworth took the injured Ward to his home in a mostly unconscious condition. After being seen by the doctor, he was taken to the local cottage hospital where he died at 11.0am on the following day from a fracture at the base of his skull. The coroner's inquest was held in Wirksworth Town Hall the same evening.

Rowland Swift of 8 Steeple Grange, a platelayer for the Midland Railway, said that he was going down the hill about 100 yards in front of Samuel Bateman at 5.45am[3]. He heard Bateman shouting *'come here'*. He went back and found that he had Ward in a sitting position in the roadway. Bateman told him that Ward had knocked him down, but was too shocked to say anything more. He could see that Ward was badly injured. His bicycle was in the road near his side. Swift said that he and a man named Conquest helped to put Ward in the mail motor and he returned with him to Steeple Grange.

Samuel Bateman, who lived at 89 Cromford Hill, said that while crossing the road to the right to get to the footpath, which he generally did at that point, he heard a rush, but before he could turn he was struck by Ward. The force of the collision knocked him down and he hurt his right hand. He was also cut in the leg and on his left arm. He did not know what struck him until he saw Ward lying in the middle of the road.

---

[1] See cover photograph.

[2] Charles records the train as the 8.55am from Manchester. This was due at Whatstandwell at 11.4am.

[3] Swift was presumably walking. Samuel Bateman is mentioned in Section 2 page 28 and Appendices "I" and "J".

Bateman said that he recognised that Ward was a railwayman because of his uniform. He could tell that he was in a serious state and raised him to a sitting position. In reply to a question from the coroner, he said that he had heard no bell, just a rushing sound. An inspection of the bicycle by the police found it to be in perfect working order.

The jury returned a verdict of *'accidental death from a fall from a bicycle'*.

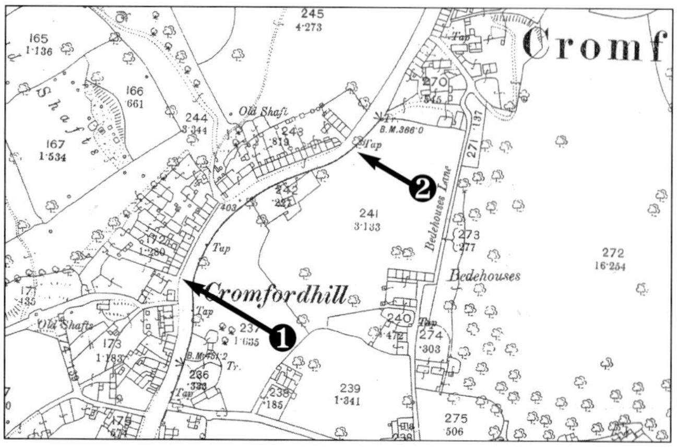

Left: A view looking down Cromford Hill c.1910. This does not really show the steepness of the hill at this point, but it will be noted that there was a pavement on only one side.
Right: An extract from the 25" to a mile map for 1922 showing part of Cromford Hill. Arrow 1 shows where the photograph on the left was taken, while arrow 2 is where it is believed that John Ward's accident took place.

APPENDIX "S"
THE DEATHS OF TWO PASSENGERS AT AMBERGATE STATION

At 7.38pm on Tuesday 14th March 1916, Frank Clayton Mason, a 40-year old fruiterer who lived at South Parade, Matlock Bath, was knocked down and killed by the 7.20pm Derby to Manchester passenger train as it entered Ambergate station.

According to his father, Alfred William Mason, a wholesale fruit merchant from Chesterfield, his son was addicted to drink and *'had not done much recently'*. However, he had recently had a 3-week period working as a market gardener at Bedford. His father had found him the work *'to get him away from home and break with old associates'*. Unfortunately, he had met with an accident and had returned from Bedford 10 days previously.

On the day of the accident Mason had told his wife that he was going to Derby, but went to Sutton-in-Ashfield and Mansfield Woodhouse instead, probably to see if he could get money from his brothers who lived in those towns. When he left Sutton-in-Ashfield he was said to be worse for drink, and after his later journey to Mansfield Woodhouse *'quite drunk'*. His brother last saw him at around 5.55pm when he caught his train bound for home[1].

William Hemmings, the Foreman Porter at Ambergate saw Mason on the bridge from platform No.4, when he was asked if there was time to get a drink before the train left for Matlock Bath. He was told that the train was due to depart in 6 minutes. Hemmings then accompanied Mason over the boarded crossing to platform No.1, from where his train would depart. They walked about 10 yards along the platform, then Hemmings left to perform other duties. He remarked that Mason smelt strongly of drink, but could walk alright.

Five minutes later as Hemmings was announcing the arrival of the train, he heard an unusual grinding noise from the engine, but did not take particular notice of it as unusual noises were often heard on the curve. However, after the train had departed he walked along the platform to where he had heard the noise to satisfy himself that there was nothing on the line, but on reaching that point found Mason's body. His feet were near the platform, with the remainder of his body in the 4-foot, practically cut in two.

George Mahoney, the driver of the 7.20pm from Derby said that he never saw or felt anything unusual as the train entered the station at between 6 and 8mph. He did not hear of the accident until later and found no traces of blood on the engine when he examined it.

---

[1] His journey to Ambergate would have involved three trains – 5.59pm Mansfield Woodhouse to Mansfield (arr. 6.3pm), 6.30pm Mansfield to Pye Bridge (arr. 6.58pm), and 7.8pm Pye Bridge to Ambergate (arr. 7.25pm).